Stars in God's sky

'Those who turn
many
to righteousness
shall shine
like the stars
of heaven
for ever and ever'

(Daniel 12:3).

Stars in God's sky

Faith Cook

PUBLISHING WITH A MISSION

EP BOOKS
Faverdale North, Darlington, DL3 0PH, England

e-mail: sales@epbooks.org
web: http://www.epbooks.org

EP BOOKS USA
P. O. Box 614, Carlisle, PA 17013, USA

e-mail: usasales@epbooks.org
web: http://www.epbooks.us

First published 2009
Second impression 2010

British Library Cataloguing in Publication Data available

ISBN-13   978-0-85234-696-9   ISBN 0-85234-696-4

All Scripture quotations, unless otherwise indicated, are taken from the New King James Version. Copyright © 1979, 1980, 1982 by Thomas Nelson, Inc. Used by permission. All rights reserved.

Printed and bound in the US by Versa Press Inc.

Contents

Illustrations

* With grateful thanks to the Evangelical Library
† With grateful thanks to Dr Penny Dickson

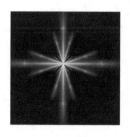

John Foxe

and his *Book of Martyrs*

John Foxe, author of the Book of Martyrs,
first published in English in 1563,
has been praised and vilified alternately, according
to the perspective of the critic. But more recently his
account of the atrocities that took place under Queen
Mary I has been verified by careful historians. Its
influence on English history has been profound.

John Foxe
(1517-1587)

and his *Book of Martyrs*

At midday on 31 October 1517 a German monk was to be seen hammering something to the door of the Castle Church in Wittenberg. It proved to be a list of ninety-five items which Martin Luther wished to have debated, an open challenge to the corruptions which he had observed in the Catholic Church of his day. The issue sparking off such a reaction was the fraudulent sale of indulgences, supposedly allowing men and women to purchase remission of stay in purgatory for their loved ones, but in truth enriching the coffers of the Vatican.

Luther's action marked the beginning of the great sixteenth-century Reformation. And during that very same year a child was born in Boston, England — another whose life would promote the cause of that Reformation to an astounding degree.

A dense spiritual darkness lay on the minds of the people of England in 1517. The power of the priests was dominant and anyone offending them or suggesting that they might be misleading the people could well meet his end in the fires of martyrdom. And into a home equally shrouded by ignorance and superstition, John Foxe was born. The child suffered an early loss in the death of his father but before long his mother remarried. His stepfather, however, was both bigoted and intolerant in matters of religion and John was taught to display a similar narrowness and ritualistic zeal.

An able boy with a flair for Latin poetry, John was enrolled at Brasenose College, Oxford, in 1533 at the age of sixteen. With commendable diligence the youth applied himself to his studies, but Oxford was a melting pot of religious ideas and John Foxe would inevitably be caught up in heated discussions. In 1527, only six years earlier, Oxford scholar Thomas Bilney had been burnt at Norwich crying out 'Credo' (I believe). What was his supposed offence? He had embraced the new teaching filtering through from the Continent, maintaining that forgiveness of sins came through faith in Jesus Christ and not through the dispensation of the church. And had not Hugh Latimer, another Oxford man and one whom young John Foxe would naturally admire, also believed such things?

More than this, a translation of the New Testament into English, the work of a certain William Tyndale, had been circulating secretly since 1526 despite the efforts of the church and government to suppress it. Previously the Scriptures had been the preserve of scholars and priests, but now ordinary people could read and understand them. Perhaps it was because of this that John Foxe now decided to make divinity his principal study instead of Latin.

Then, only one year before Foxe graduated in 1537, that same William Tyndale had been strangled and then burnt at the stake at Vilvorde, near Brussels, for his endeavours in translating the Scriptures. Such events caused the young Oxford graduate much heart-searching. Why should a man be prepared to suffer like that unless he was convinced of the rightness of his cause? He must find out the truth.

At this very time, although still only twenty years of age, Foxe's academic achievements brought him the unusual accolade of a Fellowship at Magdalen College. Here he continued his studies, taking his Masters' degree in 1543. These were formative years for John Foxe. Not only did he steep himself in a study of the Scriptures, but he spent many hours tirelessly researching the history of the church from New Testament days onwards, investigating all the controversies that had rocked it and the persecutions that had been the lot of any who would not bow to the pressure of a corrupt church or hostile government.

Yet there was something else troubling the young man. Sincere and God-fearing himself, he was appalled at the hypocrisy which he discovered among many who maintained an outward religious zeal, but whose personal lives made a mockery of the things which they professed. A crisis was approaching. Night after night a candle could be seen flickering in John's window as he spent long hours poring over his books. Sometimes he spent the entire night in study. At other times he walked alone amongst the woods and fields surrounding Magdalen. Finding some hidden corner he would pour out his heart in prayer to God, often mingling his entreaties with deep sobs.

Suspicious students overheard his sighs and petitions and began to ask themselves, 'Has John Foxe been corrupted by the "new religion"?' At last, by 1545 Foxe himself became convinced in his own mind of the errors of the Catholic Church, and when questioned by his superiors as to why he no longer attended mass he gave an honest answer: it contradicted the teaching of the Word of God. John Foxe was instantly condemned as a heretic and expelled from Magdalen, losing his modest income and his lodgings.

Worse was to come. When he returned to Boston seeking refuge under his parents' roof, he was not only turned out, but disinherited, his stepfather claiming for himself any money due to John. Now the twenty-eight-year-old academic was destitute. But God was fully aware of his predicament and though friends and family stood aloof, a nobleman, Sir Thomas Lucy, offered the young man a position as tutor to his children in his Warwickshire home near Stratford-on-Avon. For almost two years John taught Sir Thomas's children and during this time he also fell in love with Agnes Randall, a girl from Coventry, soon marrying her.

However, John Foxe was being watched by those determined to ruin him. Before long he decided that it was not right to endanger his kind host and his family. He must leave the shelter of this home. Everyone knew that the old king, Henry VIII, was dying and that when young Edward, still only nine years old, came to the throne the situation for those who loved the Reformation truths would ease. So, together with his wife Agnes, John travelled to London in search of a new position.

Penniless and uncertain as to his future, John sat on the steps of St Paul's Cathedral. Unexpectedly a stranger came and sat beside him. Pressing a small sum of money into John's hand, this unknown benefactor assured him that in three days time some new opportunity would open up for him. Who that stranger was, Foxe never knew; but three days later he was offered a position in the home of the Duchess of Richmond as a tutor to not only her own, but also her brother's five children. This brother, Henry Howard, Earl of Surrey, was at that time imprisoned in the Tower of London, having fallen foul of Henry VIII. The ageing king feared that after his death Howard, a dashing and gallant young nobleman with a distant claim to the throne of England, might try to snatch the crown from young Prince Edward. To make sure he did not, Henry then ordered his execution — a last dastardly act shortly before his own death.

Henry Howard's children, Thomas, Henry, Jane, Catherine and Margaret, remained with their aunt, the Duchess of Richmond, in her Reigate, Surrey, home, with John Foxe as their tutor throughout the reign of the boy-king, Edward VI.

John Foxe

But unknown to most, this quiet and unobtrusive-looking tutor had begun to collect together all the accounts he could discover of men and women who had suffered martyrdom for the sake of their faith in Jesus Christ. After his duties with the children were complete John could be found writing up these records, checking and rechecking them for accuracy. John Foxe's famous book, known today as the *Book of Martyrs,* was beginning to take shape. He began his record from New Testament times onwards: of Stephen and then James, later followed by Matthew and Peter — the earliest martyrs of the Christian church. Soon he was chronicling the fearful persecutions under Nero with the death of the apostle Paul. On went his busy pen as he wrote of Polycarp, Ignatius, the slave girl Blandina…

Then came the grievous day in 1553 when young King Edward died at only fifteen years of age, followed by the failed attempt to put his cousin Lady Jane Grey on the throne. The embittered Mary Tudor became queen with a determination to crush the Protestant faith and bring her country back under the control of Rome and the Pope. John Foxe, together with many others, knew they were in imminent danger.

Thomas, eldest son of the executed Henry Howard, had grown genuinely fond of his tutor, and begged him not to join others who were fleeing the country. But danger was all around. Nicholas Ridley, former Bishop of London, together with the elderly Bishop Hugh Latimer and Thomas Cranmer, Archbishop of Canterbury, had already been thrown into the Tower.

At the same time prison doors had begun to swing open, releasing others whose enmity against the evangelical gospel had put them behind bars during Edward's reign. Among these was Stephen Gardiner, Bishop of Winchester, a cruel persecutor who had previously subjected both men and women to torture and fire for their faith. And one of the first men that Gardiner wished to destroy was John Foxe. Perhaps he had heard rumours of the records Foxe had been compiling. Making an apparent courtesy visit to Thomas Howard, now a young man, Gardiner asked him casually about his former tutor. Thomas was suspiciously evasive in his answer. Again and again Gardiner called. Each time he asked after Foxe. And each time Thomas' answer was the same: either his former tutor was sick, or else away. But one day Foxe actually entered the room, not knowing that the bishop was in the house. Seeing Gardiner, he speedily departed.

'And who was that?' enquired Gardiner.

'That,' replied Thomas, 'O that is my physician, not long come from the university and somewhat uncouth in his manners still.'

'I like the look of him,' Gardiner replied, 'and will send for him as soon as I have opportunity.'

It was a sinister warning, and both Thomas and his tutor knew it. Foxe must leave English shores as soon as possible.

Hasty arrangements were soon put in place for John and Agnes, who was now expecting a second child, to sail from Ipswich bound for the Continent. But no sooner had the family embarked before a violent storm tossed the ship relentlessly up and down. As it was now in imminent danger, the only solution was to return to land. But before the vessel had struggled back to shore, news of Foxe's escape had reached Gardiner. Without delay he sent messengers to Ipswich with a warrant for Foxe's arrest. Even while the ship was still at sea the house where the fugitive family had stayed was ransacked in a search for him. Clearly it could only be a matter of hours before he would be found and arrested. Urgently Foxe pleaded with the captain of the ship to set off again as soon as possible — to go anywhere, as long as he could put the North Sea between himself and the determined Bishop Stephen Gardiner.

Landing at last in France, Foxe made his way overland to Basel in Switzerland. Here the family found refuge among those who had already emigrated to escape the fury of Mary's martyr fires. To earn enough money to maintain his family John joined himself to a printer and took on the onerous task of proof-reading for him; but his main purpose was to continue writing up his *Book of Martyrs*. And as the traumatic years of Mary Tudor's reign unfolded, lasting from 1553-1558, he had abundant material. Stories of untold suffering were reaching his ears: John Rogers, a well-loved preacher, burnt without mercy in February 1555, had been refused even the humanity of an opportunity to say goodbye to his wife and eleven young children. The fearful sufferings of his friend Bishop Nicholas Ridley, burnt in Oxford the following October, together with old Bishop Hugh Latimer, filled him with horror. He learnt of women: young women, pregnant women, old women, all thrown mercilessly to the fires for their refusal to attend mass or acknowledge the Church of Rome as the true church of Jesus Christ.

Foxe was greatly helped in his work by his fellow exile Edmund Grindal who had been one of young King Edward's chaplains. Grindal, who had settled in Frankfurt, collected detailed information from correspondence with friends in England, describing the sufferings endured by many in Mary's reign. He sifted through everything he received for accuracy and then passed it on to John Foxe to include in his records.

Finally in November 1558 came the death of Queen Mary. Through her agents and bishops she had sent almost three hundred brave men and women to an agonizing death at the stake. Now, with the accession of Elizabeth to the throne, England's exiles could return home in safety. John Foxe and his family travelled back during the autumn of 1559. When his former pupil, Thomas, who had now become Duke of Norfolk, heard of his old tutor's return he offered him accommodation in his palatial home near Aldersgate, London. Grateful for the provision, Foxe was also glad of such a haven where he could continue his labours undisturbed. Now he would have opportunity to interview eyewitnesses of those things he was describing and learn the details at first hand.

Appalled at the pitiless treatment of his fellow believers and determined to make public the misdeeds of a religious bigotry that perpetrated such things, John Foxe worked night and day compiling his detailed records. In a popular readable style he described the circumstances, trials and courageous testimony of these men and women who had 'loved not their lives to the death'. Who could tell in what way God might use such an account in future days? With a heart aflame with admiration and sorrow, he wrote of their dying expressions of trust in the God who could either deliver or sustain his people to the end. John Bradford's words of encouragement to young John Leaf of Kirkbymoorside in Yorkshire, as they were chained together to the same stake, ring out from Foxe's closely written pages: 'Be of good comfort, brother, we shall have a merry supper with the Lord this night.'

Neglecting his own health in his all-absorbing endeavour, Foxe toiled on; but he became so emaciated and ill-looking that friends who had not seen him for some time failed to recognize him. While living at the Duke's mansion, Foxe met Queen Elizabeth's own printer, John Daye. Here was a man also committed to the spread of evangelical truth and as eager as Foxe to reveal the atrocities of Mary's reign. Daye undertook the printing of Foxe's enormous book — no light task when every individual letter had to be set by hand. So closely did the two work together that eventually Foxe moved from the Duke of Norfolk's palace to share Daye's apartments not far from Aldersgate.

Although Foxe had brought out a Latin rendering of his great book in 1559, the English version was not ready until 1563. Eleven years had passed since he had set out on his colossal self-appointed task. John Foxe's *magnum opus* — initially in ten distinct books — bore a title, eighty-eight words in length, beginning with: *Acts and Monuments of these perilous days touching the matter of the church wherein are comprehended and described the great persecutions and horrible troubles that have been wrought...* For some time it was generally known as Foxe's *Acts and Monuments of the Church* but gradually the more memorable title of *Book of Martyrs* gained in popularity. Illustrated with graphic wood cuts, many showing the pain and triumphs of the martyrs of the faith, the book was an immediate success.

During that same year of 1563 an outbreak of the Plague swept across London. Could this be divine retribution for the horrors of Mary's reign, the panic-stricken people wondered? As the death toll mounted, Foxe gave himself to visiting and ministering to the sick and dying. A new seriousness was abroad and many were reading Foxe's work. So too were his critics. The easiest way to destroy the book was to claim that its contents were inaccurate, biased and exaggerated. An early critic of John Foxe's *Book of Martyrs* was Nicholas Harpsfield, one-time secretary for the persecuting Bishop Edmund Bonner, but then ending his days in the Fleet Prison.

Black letter edition of 1641 of *Acts and Monuments*,
believed to have been the only book besides the Bible that
John Bunyan had when in prison.

Seething with anger, Harpsfield took up his vitriolic pen and wrote a thousand pages of scorching words against the publication, calling it 'a farrago of lies'. These so-called martyrs were nothing but 'athletes of Satan', he maintained, together with a variety of other insults. But the people who had lived through the terrible events which Foxe described knew only too well that he wrote the truth.

The Jesuits too picked faults with the *Book of Martyrs,* and doubtless in a work of that size there were bound to be small errors. But the criticisms were counter-productive. They drove Foxe back to his sources to check and recheck every detail and to add extra information that was coming to light. In 1570 the diligent scholar was ready with his second edition. Published in two massive volumes, each fifteen inches by twelve, this edition became so popular that the Anglican convocation, an assembly of representatives from that church, ordered copies to be chained to every cathedral church in the country, next to the copy of the Bible. Now even the poorest literate man in the land could read for himself the story of the sufferings of Christ's church, not just in his own day, but since earliest times.

Gentle and kindly, Foxe was known for his generosity to the poor. The story is told of the day he visited his friend John Aylmer, once Lady Jane Grey's tutor and then Bishop of London. On leaving the bishop's palace, Foxe found himself surrounded by a group of men and women destitute of every basic necessity of life. Moved with pity, he returned to Aylmer and begged a loan of £5 — a considerable sum of money at the time. This he distributed among these needy people. When the bishop asked for a return of his loan Foxe replied sagely, 'I have laid it out for you and have paid it where you owed it — to the poor people that lie at your gate.' Aylmer was reportedly gracious enough to thank Foxe for his generosity on his behalf.

Two further editions of his *Book of Martyrs* were published during Foxe's life and by the time of his death in 1587 his work had gained a unique status. To be republished many times in the years that lay ahead, it had an unrivalled effect on the Elizabethan church and on into Stuart times. It brought about a dread of Catholicism and particularly of a Catholic monarchy, a fear which shaped English politics throughout the seventeenth century and beyond. Archbishop Laud — a cleric whose strong leanings towards the Church of Rome dictated his policies — was so afraid of the book that he had it banned during his primacy in the 1630s.

Available once again after the Civil War, Foxe's *Book of Martyrs* was the only reading material apart from the Bible that John Bunyan took into prison with him. For twelve years he was shut away in the dank and fetid atmosphere of Bedford jail, and his constant meditation on the sufferings of others helped him to endure his own. It is therefore fitting that Bunyan's own book *The Pilgrim's Progress* should be classified with John Foxe's *Book of Martyrs* as one of the two works that have moulded a nation's psyche to a marked degree.

Republished in 1684 in three huge volumes (its ninth edition), each book measured eighteen inches in height and contained nearly 1000 pages. Foxe's work could be found in many a home during the next two centuries, along with the Bible and *The Pilgrim's Progress*.

It would be strange if such a book did not have its critics, and certainly John Foxe has had his share, not only in his own day but on many occasions since. The most sustained attacks came in 1837 from the pen of S. R. Maitland, librarian at Lambeth Palace, who alleged that lies were supplied to Foxe as he compiled his accounts and therefore the work was untrustworthy. For many decades following Maitland's publications, Foxe was discredited as a reliable historian until the 1940s when J. F. Mozeley, an able scholar, began to investigate Foxe's veracity.

He surprised the critics by his discovery that the old historian was amazingly accurate. His work has reinstated Foxe's *Book of Martyrs* as a unique record, both of pre-Reformation church history and of the Tudor period. John Foxe experienced many sorrows and hardships in his life: disinherited, destitute, exiled and homeless, yet he persevered in his trust in God and with his great endeavour. One of his sons, Samuel, was initially a disappointment to John and Agnes. Rebelling against his

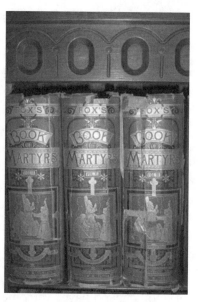

Foxe's three-volume
Book of martyrs

father's standards and wishes and dressing like a young dandy, he travelled the Continent. When he returned, his father did not recognize him. 'Who are you?' he had asked, and learning that it was Samuel he exclaimed in dismay, 'Oh my son, what enemy of thine has taught thee so much vanity?' Expelled from Magdalen College for his conduct, Samuel eventually sobered up and to him posterity is indebted for many details of his father's life. A further sorrow shook John Foxe when his former pupil and kind benefactor Thomas, Duke of Norfolk, was caught up in a plot against the Queen, purposing to put Mary Queen of Scots on the English throne instead of Elizabeth. His execution in 1572 was the sad but predictable result of such treason.

Joys too were his as Foxe saw the astonishing popularity of his *Book of Martyrs;* doubtless he would also have felt a glow of satisfaction as Charles Howard, another of his former pupils, went on to achieve national accolades in his role as Lord High Admiral of the English fleet. Foxe's death in 1587 meant that he did not live long enough to know of all of his protégé's successes, and of his part in the defeat of the Spanish Armada in 1588. But he would doubtless have known that Francis Drake had taken a copy of the *Book of Martyrs* to sea with him to wile away the long hours, and that he attributed the success of some of his naval exploits to Foxe's prayers.

John Foxe's work lives on: almost four hundred and fifty years since it was first published, it is still reprinted with added material of some of the more recent sufferings of Christian men and women. In our day when persecution is as remorseless as ever and even more widespread, the records of endurance of past days can nerve and strengthen us, for as Christ himself told his disciples, 'In the world you will have tribulation; but be of good cheer, I have overcome the world' (John 16:33).

Paul Greenwood and Jonathan Maskew

Mr Grimshaw's men

When revival broke out in Haworth in 1744, William Grimshaw found himself overwhelmed by the demands on his time and strength as he preached and counselled. Two remarkable laymen, both of whom would later become John Wesley's itinerant preachers, became his chief assistants in the work, becoming known as 'Mr Grimshaw's men'. Both would suffer the mindless persecution so often the lot of such preachers at the time.

Paul Greenwood and Jonathan Maskew

Mr Grimshaw's men

Seventeen-year-old Paul Greenwood was kneeling in the barn at his father's farm. How long he had knelt there he could not say. One thing only filled his mind. He must plead for God's forgiveness and mercy for his sins. For some months he had been deeply troubled about those things that marred his life and especially after he had listened to the fiery preaching of William Grimshaw, the curate of Todmorden in West Yorkshire at that time. Paul had spoken to the curate privately, but it seemed that even Grimshaw himself had not been able to help him for he too appeared uncertain and troubled about his own spiritual state.

Not long after this, Paul discovered a small pamphlet with a very long title written by a Robert Seagrave. It pointed a way of hope for men and women burdened by their sins. Avidly he turned its pages, and as he read he knew that this pamphlet held the answers to his urgent need. Without delay he looked for some quiet place where he could pray. The barn seemed the best solution. Hour after hour Paul knelt there in the semi-darkness, crying out to God to have mercy on him. As time passed, his father began to worry about his son's whereabouts. At last he decided to search for Paul, looking through all the outhouses. Hearing sounds coming from the barn, the farmer stood irresolute on the threshold peering into the darkness. Then he entered, and as his eyes grew accustomed to the half light, he was amazed at what he saw. Unaware of his father's presence, Paul continued praying. While he stood watching the boy an overpowering sense of his own sins forced him to his knees beside his son. He too began praying.

Soon Paul's mother became increasingly concerned about her husband and son. Where could they be? She too searched and eventually discovered them in the barn. Tears coursed down her cheeks as she saw them there and before long she knelt in the hay with them, pouring out her heart to God in prayer for his mercy. It was not long before Paul's brother and sister, alerted by the cries coming from the barn, joined the rest of the family. Together the whole Greenwood family mingled their cries and tears, until each one was assured of God's compassion and forgiveness.

With gladness and relief, Paul Greenwood was anxious to share his new-found joys with the curate, William Grimshaw, and to lend him the pamphlet that he had found so helpful. For seven years Grimshaw had been striving to please God by his good works — and had failed. But in 1741, not long before his young friend Paul Greenwood and his family had prayed together in the barn, he too had at last received that assurance of acceptance with God that had so long eluded him. In the curate's case it had been by reading a book, discovered seemingly by chance, written by the great theologian of the previous century John Owen. Entitled *Justification by Faith,* this book had brought light and understanding to his soul. Now, as he heard

Paul Greenwood's news, he was able to rejoice with him and his family with a full heart.

Not long after this, Grimshaw applied for a new appointment. The curacy in Haworth was vacant. Haworth lay eight miles from Todmorden and only two miles from Ponden End where Paul and his family lived. Perched high up on the edge of the moors, Haworth was no easy assignment. John Newton would later describe the people to whom Grimshaw came as 'wild and uncultivated, with little more sense of religion than their cattle'. But William Grimshaw was the right person for such a situation. Burly and resilient, with a personality well suited for handling his rough parishioners, Grimshaw was God's chosen man for a work of astounding usefulness during the next twenty years. And Paul Greenwood's support and contribution to that work was so marked that he soon became known as 'Mr Grimshaw's man'.

William Grimshaw

Attendance at the parish church was sparse when Grimshaw arrived in Haworth in May 1742, but, undaunted, he began to preach that same gospel which had transformed his own life and Paul Greenwood's as well. People started to come from near and far to listen to the curate's passionate appeals to the conscience and to his fearsome denunciations against their sins. 'He frequently rolled with thunder,' recalled one hearer, but added that he 'mingled tears like the Redeemer's over Jerusalem with his severity'.

Before long the numbers wishing to hear the preaching which was revolutionizing lives in Haworth and beyond had swelled to such an extent that they could no longer be accommodated in the church. 'My church began to be crowded, insomuch that many were obliged to stand out of doors,' reported Grimshaw. Torn with anxiety over their spiritual needs, people of all ages were waiting to speak with Grimshaw. Soon it became clear that he urgently needed help. And one young man to whom he turned was Paul Greenwood, now in his early twenties.

Haworth Church in 1756

During these years of revival, especially between 1744 and 1747, Paul gave himself unsparingly to helping William Grimshaw. But he was not William Grimshaw's only assistant. Jonathan Maskew, aged thirty-two at this time, had a story as surprising as Paul's own. Born into an impoverished home in Bingley, West Yorkshire, and benefiting from only limited education, Jonathan was as mischievous, if not more so, as any other boy. But there was one important difference. The youth's misdeeds distressed his conscience. Night after night he would toss sleepless on his bed, thinking over the day's sins and wondering if there was any way of forgiveness. In his ignorance he had a distorted view of God and no clear understanding of how he might be approached. His parents were godless, and could give their son no spiritual guidance, nor did he receive any help from the pulpit of the parish church in Bingley. But God can enlighten the heart by his Holy Spirit without external means if he so wishes, and it would appear that Jonathan Maskew learned the way of forgiveness by the sacrifice of Christ with little human help.

With heart aflame he began to tell his friends and neighbours of the truths that he had discovered. But he soon found that few wished to hear. So angry were his parents at the supposed disgrace brought on the family by Jonathan's new religious ideas that they turned him out of the home. Not long after this, William Grimshaw heard of the young man's predicament. With typical generosity, the large-hearted curate of Haworth invited Jonathan to live under his roof in the parsonage known as Sowdens. In return Maskew would cultivate the glebe land surrounding his new home; added to this, the zealous young man was to assist him in counselling and encouraging some of the troubled people who crowded round Grimshaw seeking spiritual help.

Gradually William Grimshaw, schooled as he was in all the protocol of the Established Church with its antipathy to laymen preaching and teaching, found that he could not manage without the help of men like Paul Greenwood and Jonathan Maskew. In one year he could count at least one hundred and twenty men and women who had been powerfully converted. So dividing his parishioners into small groups, he appointed both Maskew and Greenwood to oversee these 'home groups', teaching and exhorting the people. A visitor to Haworth describes the situation:

> Grimshaw acknowledges that he has had a great deal of assistance from two laymen in his parish, who, with his approbation, expounded the scriptures and gave exhortations to great numbers, who almost every day attend on them in private houses; and more than once he told me with an air of pleasure, that he verily believed that God had converted as many by their services as by his own.

Soon the gifts and zeal of these two young men marked them out for a wider ministry than Haworth alone. And Grimshaw was big-hearted enough to see that he must let them go. While appealing to John Wesley to send him more helpers to take the place of Maskew and Greenwood as the work of God spread over much of the north of England, these two could be found preaching ever further afield.

Circumstances for lay preachers were hard indeed. Even ordained men like the Wesleys and Grimshaw were sometimes severely manhandled by hostile crowds, but laymen fared far worse. The fearful treatment meted out to Maskew as he preached in Yeadon near Leeds makes horrific reading. Surrounding his makeshift pulpit, the crowd, inflamed by alcohol, seized the preacher, stripped him of his garments, and dragged him along a gravel path until his back was lacerated and bleeding. One particularly vicious man decided to rid the area for ever of one who disturbed them by denouncing their sins. Tying a handkerchief around the injured man's neck, he all but strangled him, until a merciful passer-by intervened.

On another occasion, as he preached in a house in the same area, the violent mob, armed with sticks, stones and a pistol, determined that this time they would kill Maskew. But unexpectedly a storm, furious in its proportions, broke out with thunder, lightening and torrential rain. Seizing his moment to escape as his persecutors cowered under hedges, Maskew leapt out of a window. Soon a hue and cry was raised. Pistol shots were fired as the angered crowd gave chase. In the dark and confusion of the storm, Maskew managed to throw off his pursuers and escape. Doubtless William Grimshaw encouraged the

Unruly mob

courageous young man, for he too had suffered violent abuse on several occasions, most particularly at Roughlee, near Colne, in 1748.

Not many months passed before John Wesley himself heard of the noble endurance of Jonathan Maskew and asked Grimshaw to release him for yet wider preaching. 'Mr Grimshaw's man' was to be found preaching in Newcastle in 1752 and then in many different parts of the country. After many years of travelling from place to place, Maskew eventually returned to the Haworth area, but not before 1763 when William Grimshaw himself had died. Here he gave himself to ceaseless toils, building up many in the faith, some of whom had been the fruits of his early ministry.

Marrying the widow of one of William Grimshaw's most notable converts, he continued his punishing round of preaching. But after some years he began to feel the physical cost of all the hardships he had suffered. Before long he was forced to give up his itinerant ministry and confine himself to preaching to those who crowded to his house. 'I have been in the service of a good Master for fifty years,' said the old preacher not long before the end of his life, 'and now I am more in love with his service than ever; and I see no need of altering any of the doctrines which I first preached when the Lord called me into his vineyard.' Many were the expressions of love to Christ which marked his final days: 'O that name, Jesus! How sweet it is!' he would exclaim. Then with an expression of unutterable joy in his eyes, he turned to his son and exclaimed, 'Look, James, look.' James could see nothing, but moments later the Saviour had taken this valiant Christian beyond the rage of men to a better world at the advanced age of eighty.

Paul Greenwood did not remain long with William Grimshaw either. When the resolute and tireless curate of Haworth first met John Wesley in 1747, it would appear that he told him about the young man converted so remarkably together with all his family in the barn. He must have shared his estimate of Greenwood's gifts and usefulness as both a preacher and an exhorter. Only months later we find Wesley requesting Greenwood, who had probably never travelled beyond the bounds of Yorkshire, to evangelize far off in Dublin. With courage he set off and was among the first Methodist preachers, apart from the Wesley brothers and John Cennick, to visit Ireland.

The risks were enormous, the people volatile, and a crowd whipped up to fury by the parish priest could easily kill a defenceless preacher. An early report of Greenwood's preaching has survived in the records of the times. A certain Samuel Handy was persuaded against his will by his newly-converted sister-in-law to go to Dolphin's Barn and hear this 'upstart preacher', as Greenwood was regarded. Fearful of being pick-pocketed, Handy hesitated, but at last agreed to go. As he entered Dolphin's Barn, he discovered a group of poor yet joyful-looking people awaiting the arrival of the preacher. Later he recorded his impressions:

> Soon a tall thin man in plain black clothes with dark hair entered and took possession of the pulpit. He was Paul Greenwood, a native of Haworth, who had just entered the itinerancy; a man of great simplicity and uprightness of heart, and distinguished by great seriousness, heavenly-mindedness and close communion with God.

Samuel Handy stared at the young preacher in amazement. No wig, no gown, no clerical bands — none of the usual paraphernalia of a cleric. What sort of preacher was this? Further surprises awaited him when Greenwood gave out a hymn. With full hearts the congregation sang out the words — doubtless one of Charles Wesley's compositions. 'How wonderful,' thought Handy, 'that so despicable a people should sing so delightfully!' Greenwood's prayer came from no book of written prayers, Handy noticed, and was full of such warmth and liberty with the God of heaven, that the man was thrilled, and eager to listen with ready heart to the preaching. This was 'accompanied with such light and power', that the critical listener found himself saying of the Methodists, 'This people shall be my people, and their God shall be my God.'

Doubtless Grimshaw was glad to see Greenwood back in Haworth in 1748 to assist him with the 'Haworth round' — a misnomer for a vast track of the north of England stretching initially from Chester, near the Welsh border, to Hull in the east, a distance of about one hundred and thirty miles across rough and often trackless terrain. In addition to regularly preaching in his own pulpit in Haworth, Grimshaw could record weeks when he had preached thirty times as he travelled parts of

View over Haworth, West Yorkshire

'the round' on horseback. Tirelessly Paul Greenwood too rode to the distant outposts of this extensive circuit, to reach unevangelized areas and to form new 'societies' of believers.

Again between 1750 and 1751 Greenwood was back on home territory. Entries in the circuit book for the area, recording all expenditures of society funds, list that Paul Greenwood received one shilling 'for washing clothes'. This suggests that the rough crowds had rolled the preacher in the mud — a regular occurrence — soiling his clothes.

Paul narrowly escaped with his life in the Yorkshire Dales as he was confronted with a mob, baying for blood. Only the intervention of his friends saved him from death. At other times the rabble confined themselves to interrupting the services until the preacher found it nearly impossible to continue. Even twenty years after he began his travels as an itinerant preacher it was the same. In Sheffield in 1765, young thugs used to provoke the congregations in all possible ways. Girls had their dresses ripped with knives or scissors, while men were pushed into the River Don. Sometimes a ruffian in disguise managed to join the hearers. Under his outfit he hid an unfortunate cockerel which he tortured until the bird drowned the preacher's voice with its piteous cackles. Ejected from the building, these mischief makers climbed up to a skylight near the pulpit and mimicked the preacher in full sight of the congregation.

Despite everything, Paul Greenwood, well taught by William Grimshaw, held on his course. One who worked with him could say: 'He was a man of a truly excellent temper and exemplary behaviour. He was constantly serious, but not sad: he was always cheerful, but not light.' In 1763 Paul lost his lifetime friend and mentor, Grimshaw, who died at only fifty-four after contracting typhus fever while visiting a sick parishioner. 'My last enemy is come,' declared Grimshaw when his friend and fellow preacher Benjamin Ingham visited him as he lay dying. 'The signs of death are on me, but I am not afraid — No! no! blessed be God, my hope is sure, and I am in his hands.'

Even if Paul Greenwood had not been able to visit Grimshaw on his deathbed, he would have heard of his courageous words spoken so soon before he left his tremendous gospel labours. Suffering intense pain, he could yet declare, 'I am as happy as I can be on earth and as sure of glory as if I were in it.' This noble example must have prepared Paul himself for a day, soon to come, when he too would be taken from his toils to a world where peace reigned and all evil was banished for ever.

Only three years later, not long after being appointed to the Manchester circuit in 1766, Paul caught an infection from which he died at the early age of forty-two. Perhaps his constitution was prematurely worn with the constant travel and unrelenting mob violence. A friend who watched by him could say of him, 'He was one of the most sincere and upright men I ever was acquainted with... He had been a blessing wherever he had laboured.' Delirious during much of his illness, Paul's mind cleared just before the end and the last night of his life was spent in constant prayer. As the early morning sun began to lighten the room where he lay, he was heard to murmur, 'Another sun shall arise; Christ the Sun of Righteousness with healing in his wings.' And these words were his last. That very morning Paul's old mother, converted on the same day as her son as she prayed in the barn, also died. As John Wesley commented when he heard of the loss of Paul Greenwood: 'He could ill be spared; but he was ready for the Bridegroom.'

Wesley had once said, 'Our people die well,' and in the lives of William Grimshaw and of 'his men', Jonathan Maskew and Paul Greenwood, this was abundantly true.

Susanna Harrison

songs in the night

*Susanna Harrison, a young
semi-literate woman, was converted
on what all thought to be her deathbed.
Making a partial recovery, she discovered
that she had an unexpected gift
for writing verse.*

Susanna Harrison
(1752-1784)

songs in the night

When Susanna Harrison was born in Ipswich in 1752, England was a land of sharp contrasts. The well-to-do thrilled to the strains of Handel's *Messiah,* lounged around in the London coffee houses listening to the outpourings of the wits of the day, or sat enthralled in the Drury Lane Theatre, London, marvelling at the performances of the actor, David Garrick. Meanwhile the poor lived in squalid circumstances, struggled to feed their large families, or succumbed to the intoxicating power of cheap gin to obliterate their miseries.

Religiously too the nation was one of contrasts. The Evangelical Revival of the eighteenth century, while bringing the gospel of God's mercy to some people, had not touched the country as a whole. In many places men and women lived their entire lives without any knowledge of the truth. Isaac Watts, the hymn-writer, had died in 1748, four years before Susanna was born, and Philip Doddridge had died only the previous year in 1751. Although John and Charles Wesley's itineraries did not take them as far east as Ipswich, the town was privileged beyond many for it had a long history of Independent or Congregational churches where a warm evangelical message was preached.

Susanna came from a large family — a family dependent entirely on her father's meagre earnings. But with his sudden death the Harrisons were plunged into poverty. Any education Susanna had previously enjoyed finished abruptly, and although she had mastered the ability to read, she was still unable to write. As soon as she was considered old enough she was obliged to earn what little she could in order to support her mother and the younger children. She probably worked as a maid for some better-placed family from the age of eight.

We know for certain that at the age of sixteen she was employed in one such home in the Ipswich area: cleaning, washing laundry and performing any other menial tasks required of her. But this home was different from most. For now she was also expected to attend a place of worship each Sunday morning, accompanying the family she served.

For Susanna this was her first experience of church attendance. From her later remarks it is clear that neither she, nor any in her family, had any previous knowledge of gospel truths. But God had unusual purposes for this poor servant girl; these circumstances meant that she was now regularly hearing a biblical message of hope and forgiveness for those who cast themselves on the mercy of God in Christ. Sunday by Sunday, as she listened to the preacher, Susanna became increasingly concerned about her own spiritual condition. She now knew that unless she changed her ways, she was unacceptable in God's sight and if she died in her present condition she would find herself cast away from him for ever. Back in her attic room as she pondered these things she wept secretly over her sins.

Yet despite her concern, she seemed unable to grasp the way of forgiveness.

Sometimes Susanna's longing became intense: if only she could know that her soul was secure — nothing else seemed to matter. But at other times she would push such thoughts to the back of her mind, becoming light-hearted and flippant once more. Then something happened which changed everything. When she was twenty she became seriously ill. At first she was cared for by the family she served; but when it became clear that her condition was life-threatening and that nothing more could be done for her, Susanna was carried back to her own family home. No one expected that the young woman would live for more than a few days at most.

The pastor of the Independent church which Susanna had been attending lived quite near to her home. Concerned at hearing that the servant girl had been brought back to her family and was not expected to live, he called to see her. He found Susanna lying on the couch, very weak and dejected in spirits. Kindly he asked her what the doctor thought of her condition. 'He fears I am dying,' replied Susanna honestly, 'and I too have given up all hope of living.'

Then the pastor probed a little deeper. 'What then are your thoughts about the world to come?'

'I am in the dark about it,' she replied, but then added, 'if I thought it would go well with me in eternity, I could gladly die, for I have for some time seen the emptiness of this world.'

'I have noticed how serious and attentive you are at public worship,' observed the pastor. 'Do you understand the way a sinner may be accepted by God?'

'Yes, I do know about the way but if only I knew that I was *in* the way, I could die at peace in my mind.'

'Why have you not spoken to me or to anyone else of these things before?' enquired her visitor gently.

'I was not able,' replied the sick woman simply, 'but now, Sir, seeing I have told you how things are with me, could you come and visit me as often as you can while I am still here, for it cannot be for long. And O, pray for me that I may know Jesus Christ and his precious salvation so that it may go well with me after death!' Exhausted, Susanna fell silent, as she sank back on her couch. Realizing she could not speak to him any more, the pastor prayed with her and then left, promising to return as soon as he could.

Some days passed before he was able to visit Susanna again, but when he came he found that her condition had deteriorated further. She had been carried upstairs to her bed and few thought she would ever come down again. Going straight to the point, her visitor asked whether her thoughts about spiritual things had changed at all. The answer he received was gratifying. 'A little better, through mercy,' replied Susanna. 'I am beginning to see some glimmer of hope that, wretched and unworthy as I am, I may yet obtain the favour of God through Christ. I do want to look to him alone who can save to the uttermost.' Then turning her gaze on her visitor she begged again with all the strength she could muster, 'O please, kind Sir, pray that God would give me some token of his love before I die, some pledge that even I may yet obtain mercy so that I may be able to say, "He has loved me and given himself for me."'

Such words amazed the pastor. Although uneducated in human terms, this young woman had surely been taught by God and was one whom he was preparing for salvation. It happened to be a Saturday evening and with Sunday ahead he could not stay long and so after a little further conversation he rose to go, promising to call again the following day. True to his word, he called back on Sunday afternoon — a visit he would never forget.

Weak as she was, Susanna's face was bright with hope. 'I have good news for you,' she declared. 'God really does hear and answer prayer! I have found what I longed for — now I can die in peace.'

'Tell me more,' replied her pastor, full of gladness. Susanna's account was simple yet gratifying:

> About four o'clock last night as I lay sleepless, grieving over my sinfulness and guilt, the Lord in his pity and mercy gave me the faith to look to the blood of sprinkling and I was helped to lay hold on Jesus as my only Saviour — what grace, what mercy to a sinful worthless woman!

'You prayed last night that I might have a good Sunday today,' continued Susanna; 'and such a Sunday I have had as I never expect to have again in this world, for I know I cannot live another week. Every moment I can feel my body failing more and more, but God, blessed be his name, is the strength of my heart and my portion for ever. "Lord, now let your servant depart in peace for my eyes have seen your salvation."'

Then the pastor had another surprise. Quite unexpectedly Susanna broke out into such heartfelt praise to the Saviour, with words of such amazing depth and beauty, that he could only listen in wonder. To him it seemed that this dying woman, snatched at the last moment from unbelief, was already joining with the hosts of heaven in praising Christ!

That evening the pastor returned and this time found Susanna's youngest brother and her mother standing by the bed, both weeping bitterly for she was saying an affectionate and final goodbye to them. 'Do not weep,' said Susanna, 'you are wounding my heart. Will you grieve because I am going to be freed from sin and be made happy in God?' Then urging her brother to seek God while he had opportunity, she shook his hand with all the strength she could muster as she took her leave of him. The pastor soon left, amazed and humbled by all he had heard.

Susanna Harrison appeared to be hovering on the threshold of heaven already and to be experiencing foretastes of glory. 'Will you sing to me?' she asked a few friends soon afterwards as they gathered around her bed. 'It is so long since I have sung a hymn.' Softly the little group began to sing:

Come let us join our cheerful songs
   with angels round the throne;
ten thousand, thousand are their tongues,
   but all their joys are one.

After singing one or two other hymns her friends began to tire, but to everyone's astonishment, Susanna continued to sing, her voice low and sweet. Most amazing was the fact that the beautiful words and tunes she was singing were ones that no one had ever heard before. It seemed like music from another world, as if Susanna could already catch the songs of heaven which the redeemed are singing, and was joining in that great paean of praise. All night with strange unearthly energy she sang quietly — at intervals her family who kept watch at her bedside thought she was actually dying — her spirit slipping away to join the songs of 'the angels round the throne'.

Surprisingly Susanna lingered on the brink of eternity for a further five days. Then quite suddenly, having scarcely eaten or slept for almost three weeks, she asked whether she could have something to eat. Soon she fell into a deep sleep. It proved a turning point, for although she would never again be well, from that moment she gradually, very gradually, began to regain her strength. God had a task for Susanna yet to accomplish — and perhaps those amazing glimpses into heaven were given to her as a preparation for it.

Many weeks passed before Susanna was able to venture out once more and her great wish, so different now that her heart and mind were enlightened by the truth, was to attend the services of worship. Drawn back from the very brink of death, she had a new longing to serve the Saviour who had done so much for her. But what could a poor uneducated girl do? Her first desire was to make some record of those glorious few days when it seemed as if she had been given a preview of the glories of heaven itself. But Susanna could not even write. If she was to leave a record of these things, she must learn; there was no alternative. Painstakingly and slowly, for she was still weak and often in pain, she taught herself to write.

Yet now she faced another problem: even if she could write, how could she ever express all she had felt and heard? Then a thought flashed across her mind. Perhaps she could try to write down these wonderful impressions in verse form or even as hymns. Unknown to anyone before, or even to Susanna herself, this young woman actually possessed an outstanding natural gift — a gift of writing verse. So now, through the long sleepless nights that were so often her lot, ideas poured into her brain. Hesitantly and secretly at first, but then with growing confidence, she began to write her poems. If God had given Job 'songs in the night',[1] thought Susanna, perhaps he could help her to write her own 'Songs in the Night'. Sermons she heard, scriptures she read, longings she felt, all became subjects for her ready pen. God's free gift of grace in her extremity of need was a natural theme. Had he not brought her out from the darkness and confusion of unbelief into the light of his salvation?

No more of works I vainly boast,
    nor so employ my tongue;
Jesus alone is all my trust,
    free grace my only song.

He saw me helpless and undone,
    a rebel dark and blind,
and led me to his blessed Son
    a better way to find.

By whose rich grace alone I stand,
   kept by his mighty power,
through which I trust ere long to land
   on the celestial shore.

Then shall I leave all sin's remains,
   and view his glorious face,
and sing in more exalted strains
   the freedom of his grace.

Susanna still faced many temptations and fears, and often Satan took advantage of her physical weakness to sow doubts and anxieties in her mind:

Why, O my soul, these gloomy fears?
Why all these sighs, and groans, and tears?
O why this God-dishonouring grief?
Why all this wretched unbelief?

Though helpless in myself I lie
and lost to all eternity,
yet shall I triumph o'er the grave,
since Jesus came to seek and save.

Then let my gratitude abound —
I once was lost, but now am found;
I once was dead, but now I live:
praise, praise is all that I can give.

Remembering the celestial songs she had heard and sung when her heart had been strangely in tune with the praises of heaven, Susanna naturally wished to express her own praises to the Lamb whose death had brought her life and who was now exalted in glory:

Susanna Harrison

How worthy the Lamb on Mount Calvary slain
who triumphed o'er death and is risen again!
How worthy of blessing and glory and praise,
the highest ascriptions archangels can raise.

While on earth I remain I shall show forth his praise
and aim at his honour the rest of my days;
and when I get home to his mansion above
all heaven shall ring with the shouts of his love.

Long weeks and months of pain and weakness were yet in
store for Susanna Harrison. More than this, she grieved acutely
over the times when she was unable to attend the services of
the church. Again the natural expression of her disappointment
and loss was in the form of verse:

Why does this room so often prove
a dungeon, Lord, to me?
When will these bars of sickness move,
to set thy prisoner free?

Jesus, I long to hear thy word,
I long to feel its power,
be thou my healer, dearest Lord,
and bring the happy hour.

Deprived of public worship, she prayed that the Lord would
come even to the room where she was confined and speak his
comforts to her soul:

Visit me here, O King of kings,
with rays of light divine;
spread o'er my soul thy healing wings,
and tell me thou art mine.

And when she was well enough to leave her room once more, Susanna's gratitude was deep and heartfelt:

> What shall I render to the Lord
> who thus regards me from above;
> how shall I best proclaim abroad
> his condescension and his love?
>
> Now in that strength which he has given,
> my willing feet his courts shall tread.
> There shall I hear good news from heaven,
> and on his promised blessings feed.

The more verses Susanna wrote, the greater grew her ability. Soon she began to experiment beyond the four-line rhyming stanzas with which she had started and to try longer paraphrases of passages of Scripture. With the words of the apostle Paul in mind, 'I have learnt in whatever state I am to be content,' she wrote:

> What manly courage, what undaunted zeal
> inspired the chief, the great apostle's breast!
> He could for Jesus' sake sustain the cross
> of persecution, poverty and pain:
> the lesson of contentment he had found
> and, as a humble scholar, learnt it well...

And as we might expect she soon applied such a lesson to her own circumstances:

> But here I stand reproved — I blush with shame,
> and mourn my vile and discontented heart.
> Forgive me, O my sin-forgiving God
> that I so much dishonour thy great name.

Susanna Harrison

Mingle my woes with all-sufficient grace,
and teach me resignation to thy will.

Yet sometimes the constant pain and weakness grew almost
too great a burden even for this brave young woman. She longed
for nothing more than that God would grant her a release from
constant suffering and call her to the place where pain and
sorrow are gone for ever.

When will my sweet release be signed
To quit this house of clay?
When shall my spirit unconfined
to glory wing her way?

Make haste my days, fly faster still,
and bring me to the place,
to that delightful holy hill
where Jesus shows his face.

Why am I chained to earth so long,
exposed to every snare?
When shall I join the heavenly throng
and dwell for ever there?

Yet Susanna did not view the thought of death lightly or
without due regard to the great day of judgement which all
must face. Sometimes she was so ill that she felt death was
imminent; then she would cling to the Redeemer for his mercy
in that final hour:

My life declines, my strength is gone,
disease and pains prevail;
death threatens to arrest me soon,
my heart and flesh must fail.

Soon I must leave this body here,
soon must my soul away;
O awful thought! My soul prepare
for that tremendous day!

Jesus, on thee alone I lean,
do thou my soul prepare;
O cleanse my heart from every sin,
and fix thy dwelling there.

Every frame of mind, every trial and temptation, every joy
and fear of the Christian seemed to find its way into Susanna's
verses during the following eight years. In all probability she
was familiar with Isaac Watts' *Hymns and Spiritual Songs,*
published in 1707, but the thoughts and expressions were her
own. And still few knew anything about her ability. Then came
a day when once again the disease that was destroying her body
— a disease that her doctors could neither diagnose nor relieve
— seemed about to bring her life to a close. At twenty-eight
years of age and apparently dying, she began to think about
her book of poems, which had been growing steadily thicker
every day. It now numbered more than one hundred and thirty
pieces. Perhaps, she thought, some other suffering believer
would one day find consolation through her 'songs in the
night'. Calling her pastor to her bedside, shyly and diffidently,
Susanna entrusted her little collection to his care with strict
instructions not to show them to anyone else until she had left
this earthly scene.

We can well imagine him sitting late into the night, reading
with astonishment the verses from this gifted young woman's
pen. He may well have guessed her hidden ability for he had
heard some of the ascriptions of praise to God which she had
spoken in her former severe illness. No, he could not keep
these to himself. They would surely be of help to some other

struggling believer. As it became clear that yet again Susanna had pulled through the crisis and seemed likely to live on for a while, he had an idea. If the poems were published, the money raised from the sales could be used to support the invalid. It was certain that she would never be able to work again.

At first Susanna resisted the idea, but gradually and with some difficulty she was persuaded to agree. She feared that some might think she was seeking honour for herself. Lines she wrote at this time express her feelings:

Is this thy will — and must I be
a living witness, Lord for thee?
Must I thy wondrous love record
and spread thy praises far abroad?

Wilt thou no longer me excuse,
and wilt thou frown if I refuse?
O, let me have thy presence still,
and I'll submit to all thy will.

To thee I dedicate the whole,
thine is my heart and thine my soul;
bless what my feeble hand has wrought,
and take the praise for every thought.

Wilt thou, dear Lord, thy handmaid own?
Her offering with ACCEPTANCE crown?
Thy glory is her humble aim —
ETERNAL GLORY TO THY NAME.

So it was that in 1780 *Songs in the Night* was published anonymously, the writer only describing herself as 'A young woman under heavy affliction'. Carefully edited by her pastor, a few grammatical mistakes were ironed out from her lines, but for the most part he allowed any irregularities of expression to stand as she had written them, for they spoke eloquently of the individuality and earnestness of the writer. Even her pastor was astonished at the sales, and before long the edition had sold out with the public clamouring for more copies and more poems from this writer's hand. Added to this there was a demand to know the name of the author.

Would Susanna agree to allow her name to be made public? Certainly not at first, but after further urgent persuasions she decided to write an acrostic so that some more discerning readers might be able to guess her name. Full of epigrams and contradictory riddles, she submitted these lines:

Shall I presume to tell the world my name?
Up to this hour I glory in my shame.
So great my weakness, that I boast of might;
A fool in knowledge, yet in wisdom right,
No life and yet I live; I'm sick and well;
Not far from heaven, though on the brink of hell.
And words, and oaths and blood delight me well.

How strange! I'm deaf and dumb and lame and blind
And hear and talk and see and walk, you find.
Robbed of my dearest Friend, I'm truly poor,
Riches immense I always have in store.
I'm fed by mortals; but let mortals know,
Such is my food, no mortal can bestow:
O how I long to die and wish to live!
Now, if you can, explain th'account I give.

In 1782, therefore, a second edition was published, which included an extra eleven pages of verses, this time edited by and with a warm recommendation from Dr John Conder of Hackney, London. 'The whole seems to breathe a true spirit of

sublime devotion and the subject matter is highly evangelical,'
he commented in his preface.

So adept did Susanna become at writing in verse that she
even expressed life's trivial experiences in this way, often turning
a mundane subject to spiritual account. To one who had given
her a new dress, she wrote:

The garment that you gave me I admire,
it suits me, as I'm fond of neat attire,
and should uncertain health admit, I'll wear
this garment to the honour of your care...
When your kind hand to me the favour brought,
it led my thoughts to Jesus — as it ought...

And when she returned a copy of John Bunyan's small book,
The Heavenly Footman, to the friend who had lent it, she
wrote:

Madam: I now return your little book
and thank you for the short but pleasing look;
for though 'tis only for a trifle sold,
'tis more than worth its weight in shining gold.
It was for slothful souls at first designed,
and vastly suited my sad sluggish mind.
I read, I hope, with seriousness and care,
and highly prized the truths I met with there.

Not surprisingly yet another edition of Susanna's verse was
called for in 1784, the year that proved to be the year of her
eventual death. So great was the demand that a fourth edition
came out four years later with twenty-two further pages of
previously unpublished material. And only in 1823, after the
fifteenth edition, did Susanna Harrison's *Songs in the Night* cease
to be republished. Such astonishing popularity has even earned

Title page of 1823 edition
of *Songs in the night*

the Ipswich servant girl a place in the *Dictionary of National Biography.*

Even though she had long lived with illness and pain, Susanna's last days were hard. Unable to take any sustenance for many days before her death, she was so reduced in weight that friends said she seemed a mere skeleton at the end. Scarcely able to speak she could only whisper as she pointed upwards, 'I cannot talk, but I will soon be there.' And at last after fourteen years of suffering this courageous young woman died on 3 August 1784. Now she was granted her long desire to join the anthem of heaven, praising the Lamb for ever. Well could she sing:

All glory to the Lamb of God,
my robes are spotless in his blood;
'tis through his free and sov'reign grace
I now behold his blissful face.

She was buried in Tacket Street cemetery in Ipswich and on her gravestone a poem was written in her memory, with an exhortation to the passer-by. It ended with the words:

Her state was humble but her faith was true
And what she sung, she sung from what she knew:
Her themes, her songs were full of love divine —
Reflect — and make, like her, religion thine.

Note

1. Job 35:10.

Sidney Flack

child of revival

*Sidney Flack, born in an Essex village in 1887,
was an illiterate building labourer. But converted
to God in 1904 in an unusual work of the Spirit,
he became an avid reader and Christian worker,
living until the advanced age of 101. His life
was one of exceptional usefulness
in the service of God.*

Sidney Flack
(1887-1988)

child of revival

The village of Chrishall in Essex where Sidney Flack was born on 14 April 1887 remains much the same today as it was over one hundred years ago. On an early summer afternoon a visitor may still wander along its quiet winding lanes, past sleepy-looking thatched cottages with thick whitewashed walls. A small stream, shielded from the sunlight by tall bulrushes and low-growing trees, meanders slowly through the village and dragonflies flit busily here and there. May trees blossom profusely in the hedgerows and few man-made sounds intrude. But idyllic as Chrishall may seem to us today, life for the villagers when Sidney was growing up was tough. All week they laboured in the fields, cultivating their crops or tending their flocks. Many would then travel the seven miles to the long-established market in Saffron Walden to sell their produce.

'You will never rear him,' the doctor had told his mother soon after Sidney was born, for he was a frail infant and his grasp on life seemed tenuous at best. Much of Sidney's schooling — little enough in any case — was lost through illness and it often appeared that the doctor was to be proved right. When he left school at fourteen, his formal education finished, Sidney was still unable to read or write. Now he was expected to help the family finances and before long he found employment as a builder's labourer. Up early in the morning, he worked hard all through the day.

Despite the many hours spent in the open air, the youth was finding it difficult to sleep. Night after night it was the same, but not due to any physical condition. For Sidney had a burdened conscience. Yet he scarcely knew where to turn for help. Again and again he crept out of his bed and, regardless of the cold, knelt down on the hard floor and tried to pray. Perhaps, he thought, if he prayed long enough and earnestly enough God would eventually hear his prayers, forgive his sins and give him the peace of mind he so desperately wanted. Then climbing back into bed once more, the boy would fall asleep at last.

Village life centred on the Primitive Methodist Chapel, a small, sturdy-looking building standing on the main road through the village. First built in 1862, twenty-five years before Sidney was born, it had to be enlarged nine years later.[1] And here Sunday after Sunday Sidney would sit on one of the hard wooden pews trying to understand what the preacher was saying. Usually he would listen to the local preachers who visited the village chapel. But every winter for as long as he could remember, a horse-drawn caravan would arrive in Chrishall and a group of travelling evangelists announce preaching services to be held in the chapel each evening. For three weeks or more the evangelists preached until at last they harnessed up their faithful horse once more and headed off towards the next village.

Chrishall Methodist Church

Even though Sidney had listened to the caravan preachers for many years, their words had had little effect upon him. But then he started to become seriously concerned about his sins. Throughout the spring and summer of 1904, when Sidney was sixteen years of age, his spiritual struggle intensified. If only he could read, he thought, then he might be able to find some answers to his concerns in the pages of the Bible from which the missioners preached. And there was another problem too: Sidney was scared that if he made an open confession of faith, as he knew he should, he might become a laughing stock among the other village lads and that was something he felt he could not face.

At last the boy came to a decision — one which he hoped would both quieten his conscience and mean that he would not need to speak of his faith to his friends and associates. In November of that year he was due to visit Bridlington for a short holiday in one of the town's boarding houses. His plan was to wait until his holiday before settling the disturbing issue of his unforgiven sin. 'Then if you are away from home you will not need to say anything about your faith,' the devil cunningly whispered in his ear.

Setting off for Bridlington that November, Sidney had not forgotten his intention to deal with the matters that had been troubling his conscience. But soon after his arrival God took the initiative in this young man's life in a way that he had not anticipated. When Sunday morning came round he decided to attend the Primitive Methodist chapel in the town as he usually did at home. But on the way his attention was arrested by the sound of drums, of brass instruments and of the steady tramp of feet. Stopping to watch the band pass by, Sidney soon realized that these were Salvation Army men and women heading for their place of worship.

To his own surprise Sidney felt a strange inner compulsion to change his plans and to follow the band. Before long he found himself seated in a simple Army hall listening earnestly to the message being preached. And as he listened he began to tremble. All his sins rose up before him in dreadful array — sins with which he had long wrestled and had been unable to overcome. By the end of the service he was so agitated and distressed that he could not even put on his own coat before leaving the hall. A kindly Salvation Army man, seeing his state, had to come to his aid.

On returning to his boarding house Sidney could be found on his knees before God pleading more urgently than ever for mercy and forgiveness. And before long his anguish turned to joy as he knew at last that his sins were blotted out for Christ's sake. Now he could scarcely contain his happiness and relief. Gone were his fears of the opinions of others. He wished for nothing more than to return to Chrishall and to tell everyone about his new-found joys, and to urge his friends and all whom he might meet to seek and find that same forgiveness.

November 1904, that very month when Sidney Flack experienced God's saving power in his life, is also a highly significant date for the wider Christian Church. It is rightly celebrated as the dawn of an unusual period of God's mercy in Wales: the start of the 1904-05 Revival. Simultaneously it would seem men, women and young people began crying out to God for forgiveness of sin in places as far apart as Loughor, near Gorseinon in South Wales, and Rhos, near Wrexham in North Wales. But the fact that such a mighty work of God was beginning in Wales was quite unknown to Sidney Flack as he travelled back to Chrishall, his heart bubbling over with joy. Nor could he have known that at that very same time God was also preparing to visit his own village in an amazing way.

In all likelihood the revival of religion in Chrishall, for it was nothing less, coincided with the annual mission of the caravan evangelists. Year after year they had visited the village, coming each winter, but without any obvious effect on the lives of the people. Yet in November 1904 it was different. Now as the people were listening to the preaching, deep concern was etched on every face. For Sidney himself the joy he felt was so intense that almost seventy years later he could describe those days as though they had only just happened. During the following few months more than forty conversions were recorded in the village, mainly among the younger people, some of whom had come from neighbouring villages — an astonishing work of God in such a sparse rural community. Long after the evangelists had packed up their caravan and moved elsewhere, God continued to be at work through the regular preaching at the chapel.

Village life was transformed, for this was no short-lived burst of religious fervour which would vanish again without a trace. Indeed, it left an imprint which can still be seen today by anyone who wanders around the small graveyard at the rear of the church. From the words on the gravestones we may find clear evidence that the 'children of the revival' lived all their lives in submission to God and in his service. Engraved on the old grey stones, some half-buried in the long grass, we may read their moving words of testimony. When Esther Brand's fifty-three-year-old husband died in 1947, she chose to inscribe his stone:

Thou art with Christ and Christ with me.
In Christ united still are we.

Charles Clarke was thirty when the revival broke out and for the next fifty years lived 'A life in the Master's service'. A rough boulder marks the last resting place of another couple who 'Walked with the Lord'; while grieving parents whose youngest son was killed in action in France in 1916 could humbly inscribe his stone, 'Thy way not mine, O Lord'. Most of the converts were young people and within ten years a number would see action in the First World War. How many would die in the conflict we may never know — it is enough that God was preparing the young people of Chrishall for a better place where conflict, pain and death are excluded for ever.

Sidney Flack himself was used by God in an extraordinary way during this time. Aflame with zeal and concern for others, the sixteen-year-old spoke to all who would listen and to many who would not, urging them to seek the mercy of God while opportunity remained. On one occasion the earnest youth saw a ploughboy hard at work in one of the fields near Chrishall. Up and down the field went Sidney Pledger, guiding his horse and plough carefully along the furrow. Up and down the field beside him went Sidney Flack, pleading with him all the time to consider his spiritual destiny. At last the kindly young Christian placed one hand on the ploughboy's shoulder and begged him to delay no longer in seeking God. A week later Sidney Pledger was converted. He confessed that throughout the week he had been unable to shake off the sensation of the weight of Sidney Flack's hand upon his shoulder until he too knew his sins were forgiven.

Equally significant was the fact that this unique work of God's Spirit, like the Welsh Revival itself, stopped almost as dramatically as it had started. After the end of 1905 there were few, if any, further conversions in the village. As in any revival there were one or two whose professions of faith proved to be short-lived, but for most the work of grace accomplished in those few short months proved to be genuine, leading to years of faithful Christian living.

In keeping with the common practice among both Wesleyan and Primitive Methodists, the converts of the revival were organized into class meetings, one for men, another for women. Some thirty other men met in Sidney Flack's class, and each was encouraged to speak of what God had done for his soul — not just in conversion but during the days of the week that had just passed. Assured of complete confidentiality, problems were shared, sins confessed, and relapses grieved and prayed over. In this way, under the guidance of an older Christian, these young men and women of the revival were stimulated to continue in faithfulness and service to God.

For Sidney himself, his zeal and desire to spread the gospel at every opportunity could scarcely be restrained. Day after day he toiled at his work as a builder's labourer, but as the early Primitive Methodists had once done, no sooner had work finished before the youth was off to neighbouring villages where he would gather together any willing to listen to him and then begin to preach. Still unable to read or write he would take with him a friend or older Christian who would read the Scriptures for him. Sometimes he would walk twelve miles or more to preach at some distant village.

But Sidney longed to be able to read himself. Above all, he wished he could study the Bible. At last a kindly friend offered to teach him to read. Never could anyone have had a more eager pupil, and before long Sidney had begun to master the intricacies of the English language. Now there was no holding him back. He became an avid reader, giving long hours to reading both the Bible and any other book he could either buy or borrow. And gradually a new determination began to form in the young man's mind. He had heard of an evangelistic society called the Christian Colportage Association, whose work was to engage men who would travel from one town or village to the next selling Christian literature. Perhaps he too could become a colporteur. Then with a bicycle basket filled with challenging and helpful books and tracts he could ride out to all the villages dotted around the north Essex countryside, selling his literature and speaking to the people he met of the gospel that had transformed his own life.

In the days before Christian bookshops and church bookstalls existed to sell or distribute Christian literature, such men criss-crossed the country working long hours with sacrificial zeal to spread the gospel. Sometimes they met with abuse, but more often were greeted with interest, for the English villages were isolated and, without the media pouring information into their homes from newspapers, radio and television, men and women had little other contact with events beyond the bounds of their own village.

Applying to the Colportage Association to become one of its workers, Sidney Flack was granted his desire and soon began a work which would occupy him for much of the rest of his life. With a bold sign attached to the front of his bicycle announcing his errand, and urging people to 'Buy the Truth', he set off on his new endeavour. The sight of the eager young evangelist, his bicycle basket crammed full of books, soon became a familiar one in the villages that radiated outward from Chrishall. Elmdon, Littlebury Green, Arkesden, Stickling Green, and many more besides, greeted the young colporteur with interest. Children crowded around and begged for a story from his ever-ready fund of anecdotes. Many would stay to listen to a story from the Bible.

Sidney was particularly gifted for such work. With a natural interest in people, a bright talkative disposition, and a love of little children, he quickly won his way to the hearts of the villagers. Few could resist gathering a little money together to buy one of his books. And if they could not afford a book, he would press a tract into their hands.

Sidney, in later years, still working as a colporteur

With little other 'traffic' on the roads and lanes Sidney developed a habit that persisted through life, that of riding in the middle of the road — a habit that would prove highly dangerous in years to come.

The village of Chrishall remains a most attractive spot, a reminder of 'Old England', but two miles further south there lie two yet prettier villages — or so Sidney Flack thought. He loved to visit Langley Upper Green and its sister village Langley Lower Green and to preach in the chapel. But perhaps he had an ulterior motive for his frequent visits. For Annie Harvey, an attractive Christian girl and one of a family of twelve, lived there. But Sidney was a wise man and not one to be swept off his feet merely by a pretty face. When he had the misfortune of tearing his handkerchief — not so easily replaced then as now — he asked Annie if she could mend it for him. On his next visit to Langley Lower Green she returned his handkerchief mended so neatly that it was almost impossible to tell where it had been torn. 'That', said Sidney to himself, 'is the girl I am going to marry!' But still he waited before making any formal proposal.

Annie, who was several years younger than Sidney, had been working as a kitchen maid in the stately home of Lord and Lady Braybrooke at Audley End near Saffron Walden since the age of fourteen. So weekends were the only time when the young couple could meet. But by now the shadow of war was beginning to gather over Europe. Then on 28 June 1914 came the assassination of Archduke Ferdinand, heir to the Austro-Hungarian throne, which acted as a catalyst, pitching the nations into that fearful conflict that cost the lives of so many eager and gifted young men. A mere six weeks later, on 4 August, Britain declared war on Germany and Lord Kitchener called for 100,000 men to join the armed forces for the protection of their country. Sidney Flack, recently turned twenty-seven, was among the volunteers. Joining the Royal Engineers the young man was sent to Mesopotamia (present-day Iraq), for it was vital to protect the oil supplies so necessary for the war effort and which were under threat from Turkey. Here, after an appropriate training, he would serve his country for the next six years — with all thought of the girl he loved resolutely consigned to the back of his mind.

Although Sidney saw little action during the war years, he served his country well. Nor did he forget his passionate concern for the spread of the gospel. Day after day he could be found among the men speaking of his faith and of their own desperate need of a refuge for their souls, particularly in view of their imminent danger and death. To mark his personal cutlery Sidney engraved the words 'Saved by grace' on his knife, fork and spoon. Now there was little danger of any other soldier wishing to 'borrow' Sidney's possessions. Bemused at first by the earnest young man, the army chaplain soon began to realize that Sidney Flack's grasp of Scripture and ability to preach was greater than his own. Whether out of humility or convenience we may never know, but before long he invited Sidney to preach instead of him whenever he wished. More than this, Sidney also found opportunities to speak to some of the Bedouin peoples who lived and worked in Basra and beyond.

Not until 1920 when he was thirty-three years of age did Sidney at last return to Chrishall and claim the hand of Annie Harvey, now head cook at Audley End, as his bride. And a happy marriage it proved, with Jean, their only child, born in 1921. The couple's first home together was in Spalding, Lincolnshire, where Sidney became the pastor of a small Congregational church. But the days were hard. Recession following the Great War meant that often Sidney and Annie scarcely had enough money to provide for themselves and their infant daughter. Added to this, the senior deacon had little sympathy with the earnest Bible-centred message that Sidney preached. A mean man, he held that a pastor should receive as little money as possible. 'You get the same wages as my labourers,' he shouted, when Sidney told him that he could not manage on the pittance he was given. 'And you won't get no more,' he added for good measure. When one day Sidney nearly hit the lamp above the pulpit as he demonstrated some point during his sermon, the deacon roared out from the pew. 'You mind that lamp, Flack, it cost a lot of money.'

At last Sidney Flack knew he would have to find some other means of support. Industrious and ingenious, he decided to run a fish and chip shop to augment his income. But it was not his poverty that was the greatest problem. Liberalism was fast sweeping through the churches, dominating the pulpit and emptying the pews. In order to become an accredited minister Sidney would need to take certain examinations, and the Congregational superintendent brought him books to study that denied the inspiration of Scripture. That was too much. Sidney resigned the pastorate. What could he do now? The answer seemed clear; he would take up his work as a colporteur once more, doubtless riding the Lincolnshire roads as precariously as he had the lanes of Essex.

Never strong physically, Sidney battled against ill health for much of his life. Annie cared for him faithfully, but even her skills were baffled when her husband began to lose weight dramatically. No one knew what was wrong, and still he became more and yet more emaciated. From a healthy one hundred and eighty pounds in weight (81.65kgs) he had sunk in a mere six weeks to eighty-four pounds (38.1kgs). Now it was obvious that this humble and earnest Christian evangelist must indeed be dying. As he lay in his hospital bed Sidney opened his eyes to see that all his grieving relatives were standing around. 'What are you doing here?' was his amazed enquiry.

'We fear there is nothing else we can do for you now,' answered his nurse truthfully. 'I am not going to die,' responded Sidney with all the strength he could muster. 'God has a work still for me to do.' And he was right. Gradually, very gradually, Sidney began to regain a little strength, and soon it became clear that he was indeed likely to recover. Whether the cause of his illness was ever diagnosed we do not know, but just as soon as he was able he was back on the roads again, taking his gospel literature to all the Lincolnshire hamlets and villages.

But it had been a hard few years in Spalding: illness and poverty and the struggle against an ever-increasing liberalism in the church had brought many trials. Sidney and Annie longed to return to Chrishall once more and in 1932, when Jean was ten years of age, the family moved back to Sidney's home village. Four happy years were spent there — years which have left a permanent mark on the village, not just in gospel endeavour but in bricks and mortar. For Sidney, whose early training as a builder's labourer had given him skill and experience, built the general stores in the village and his own bungalow as well. Open-air preaching and colportage work filled up any spare moments while Annie ran the shop to support the family.

Not long before the traumatic years of the Second World War Sidney and Annie moved yet again, this time back to Lincolnshire, although not to Spalding. Holbeach St Johns, lying seven miles south of Spalding, is a small cluster of houses which may have reminded Sidney of his own village home. Certainly it was a good base for reaching some of the remote Lincolnshire villages with his Christian literature. Here they lived for the next twenty years or more and once again Sidney built a bungalow for himself and his wife, for by this time Jean was ready to leave home. It was here that Sidney was also called upon to nurse Annie through a long and painful illness until at last she was taken from the sufferings and sorrows of this world at the age of seventy-seven, leaving Sidney a lonely old man.

The years that followed may well have been among the hardest of Sidney's life. Selling his bungalow in Holbeach St Johns he found accommodation in a Christian guest house at Sutton on Sea, near Mablethorpe on the Lincolnshire coast. He lodged there during the winter months, then in the summer, when the room was needed for guests, he would visit relatives and friends. But God had a merciful and kindly provision for his elderly servant. For in April 1968 a Christian pastor, his wife and three small girls came from Wattisham in Suffolk for a holiday in the guest house. Sidney was still there at the time, and Gordon Hawkins and his wife Shirley found themselves drawn out in love and sympathy to this godly man, now over eighty years old, whose love of the Scriptures and the gospel so strongly matched their own.

Would Sidney Flack like to come to Wattisham for a short holiday? they wondered. Two months later he arrived and spent a happy eleven days with the Hawkins family. His delight in and understanding of small children soon won him a place in the hearts of the entire household. Each summer Sidney came to Wattisham when his room at the guest house was needed for other visitors. But in 1973, sick and needy, Sidney learnt that his landlady in Sutton on Sea was to remarry. He would have to move out for good.

But where could he go? Jean was married and had a family of her own and could not accommodate her old father. Would the Hawkins give him a more permanent home? It was a daring thought, but Sidney's need was great. Suffering from a severe heart condition, the eighty-six-year-old felt he had not long to live in any case. And with amazing audacity he wrote to Gordon and Shirley asking if he could possibly come and live with them.

With typical selflessness and compassion Gordon and Shirley opened their home to this elderly Christian man, offering him a room which would always be his. And one of the first things they discovered was that there was little wrong with Sidney's heart. It was the medication itself that was causing the problems. Before long Sidney's health was so much improved that he was able to keep the manse gardens in excellent order.

Disciplined, orderly and abstemious, the elderly Sidney Flack experienced some of his happiest years in the Wattisham manse. The old man's health improved to such an extent that he lived on until after his one hundred and first birthday — nearly seventeen years in Gordon and Shirley's home. Shirley was determined to treat any visitor who came under her roof as she would treat the Lord Jesus Christ himself if he had come to stay — her aim to act towards him with as much respect as she would to royalty, for, she reasoned, 'Are not all believers kings and priests to God?'

In return Sidney cared for the gardens for as long as he was able, and left an example of Christian devotion, prayerfulness and zeal which many in Wattisham still remember with thankfulness. During his final years Sidney's sight failed and this was a grievous trial to one who was so avid a reader. But Gordon managed to obtain a taped version of the

Sidney, on his 100th birthday

Scriptures for him, to which he would listen each day, and also some tape-recorded books. Even when listening he always insisted that he was still 'reading'. Sometimes Jean came to stay. As yet she had made no profession of faith, although she was the subject of her father's earnest prayers. Sidney would ask his daughter to read the Scriptures to him. With no personal love for the words she was reading, Jean would sometimes try to skip a few verses in order to shorten the reading. It was useless. 'You have left something out!' her father would interrupt. Nothing remained but to go back and read it all over again.

The end came very quietly in September 1988. Bedridden for the final weeks of life, Sidney longed to go home, and one night when Gordon slipped into his room to pray with him as he so often did, he discovered that his elderly friend had died. A hymn Sidney loved and which he chose for his funeral service spoke eloquently of his desires, now abundantly fulfilled:

We speak of the realms of the blest,
    that country so bright and so fair,
and oft are its glories confessed;
    but what must it be to be there!

We speak of its freedom from sin,
    from sorrow, temptation and care,
from trials without and within;
    but what must it be to be there!

'The gospel meant everything to Sidney Flack,' said Gordon Hawkins at the funeral service. 'His life was an example to us. Tenacious in faith, regulated, tidy, disciplined, contented, industrious, grateful and loving ...' These were high accolades indeed from one who had lived closely with him. 'And above all, he was a man who prayed,' said Gordon. How joyful he would have been to know that his daughter Jean was wonderfully converted a few months after her father's death. Such men as Sidney Flack, converted during a revival, reveal a quality of Christian living that is rare in our own day. This world is a poorer place without him.

Note

1. Now a Methodist chapel.

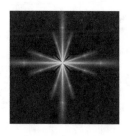

Gerhard Tersteegen

discovering
the hidden love of God

Gerhard Tersteegen, gifted German poet
who wrote some of our most evocative hymns,
was shy by nature and loved solitude.
But God called him to be a preacher
and his life was spent in the service of others
as he started a number of 'Homes for Pilgrims'.
Here Christian families could live as a community,
working and worshipping God together.

Gerhard Tersteegen
(1697-1769)

discovering the hidden love of God

A young man in his mid-twenties lay neglected and ill in his rented room. The year was 1723 and for some time Gerhard Tersteegen had been suffering violent headaches, fainting fits, high fevers and coughing. Lying on the floor of his room, he longed for someone to bring him even a drink of water to alleviate his thirst, but although others in the house knew of his condition, they would rarely concern themselves about him.

Born in November 1697 in the town of Moers, some twelve miles north of Düsseldorf, in northern Germany, Gerhard was one of the eight children born to Henricus and Conera Tersteegen. But when Gerhard was only five years old, his father, a successful merchant, died. Henricus, who had probably been involved in the manufacture and sale of linens and silks, left his family well placed financially. But in spite of this, Conera could not have found it easy to bring up her large family alone. She soon realized that her young son Gerhard was unusually gifted academically, and so decided to send him to a well-reputed school where he would receive a high standard of classical education.

Good-looking and well liked by his peers, Gerhard studied hard for ten years, achieving a working knowledge of French, Hebrew, Latin and classical literature. He delivered a fine graduation speech in Latin at the conclusion of his school course and was urged by the school trustees to continue to a university education. But his mother, who may well have been in some financial difficulty by this time, was anxious that Gerhard should be in a position to earn his living and wanted him to learn the family business instead. With this in mind Conera made arrangements for the seventeen-year-old to go to Mülheim, fifteen miles away. Here he would lodge with his brother-in-law, Matthias Brink, working as his apprentice. But Gerhard had little interest in business or money-making. A loner and inclined to be dreamy, he found such a training irksome, particularly as it gave him little time for reading and study.

Mülheim had recently been the scene of a spiritual awakening. Pastor Melchior, whose ministry in the town spanned the years 1708-1717, could describe Mülheim as a place where hymns of praise to God were to be heard from almost every home and workshop, as the people delighted to encourage each other in the faith. Because the once-vibrant life of the Lutheran Church had dwindled into legal formality those whose hearts were alive to God met together in 'conventicles', as they were called. These religious gatherings, similar to those in Scotland and England half a century earlier, were frowned upon by the church.

Before long, Gerhard found himself attracted to the conventicles and was soon profoundly touched by the message of personal salvation which he heard from the preachers. At these gatherings he met Wilhelm Hoffmann, a young man whose friendship would play an important part in Gerhard's life. Hoffmann had been a theological student, but his spiritual zeal and determination to take part in conventicles had brought on him the displeasure of his church and now he supported himself as a linen weaver, preaching whenever he was able.

Hoffmann lent Gerhard books and directed his enquiring mind towards the truths of the gospel of Christ. But although Gerhard heard many sermons from the preachers, each inviting men and women to find refuge for their souls in Christ, and warning them of a final day of judgement if they rejected such offers of mercy, he remained confused and uncertain. Half-awakened to the truth, he still groped in semi-darkness, supposing he must find a way of pleasing God by his upright life and kindly deeds to help the less fortunate.

At last in 1718, with his four-year apprenticeship finished, Gerhard set himself up in business. However, his heart was not in it, and his venture soon collapsed. Yet, far from being dismayed, Gerhard eagerly anticipated the time when he could shut himself off from all the bustle of business life and work in the quietness of his own hired rooms. In 1719 he rented a room where he installed a loom of his own and began the less arduous task of earning a living by ribbon weaving.

With his natural tendency to prefer solitude, and with a mystical streak in his personality, Gerhard was delighted that he could now devote as much time as he wished to contemplation, reading, prayer and charitable work. Behind this desire was a basic misconception, however. He thought that if, like the monks shut away in their monasteries, he could isolate himself from the babble and confusion of the religious ideas of his day, he would eventually find God and be accepted by him. Earning only a paltry living as a ribbon weaver, Gerhard toiled early and late, subsisting on the most meagre of diets: flour, water and a little milk. Despite his scant earnings he gave away as much money as he could to the needy of Mülheim-on-the-Ruhr, where he lived.

However, contrary to his expectations, this did not resolve his spiritual problems. Instead Gerhard was cast even further into a quagmire of religious doubt and mental gloom. Even worse, a Lutheran pastor lent him various books by Pietist writers and also the works of the mystic, Jakob Boehme; but these only added to Gerhard's confusion. A feeling of despair settled on his spirit and his sense of sin intensified. Even the grasp he had once attained of evangelical truth was slipping from his mind. He began to drift away from clear gospel teachings into a form of Quietism, which called upon its adherents to lead a life of stillness and contemplation, spending much time in doing good as a means of becoming acceptable to God.

For five years Tersteegen remained in this condition, sometimes hoping in the mercy of God, sometimes despairing of it. Words he wrote at this time reveal the distress that often clouded his spirit:

> Lost in darkness, girt with dangers,
>   round me strangers,
> through an alien land I roam...
> Outward trials, bitter losses,
>   inward crosses,
> scarce a spark of faith and hope.
> Bitter tears my heart oft sheddeth
>   as it dreadeth
> I am past thy mercy's scope.

Even his friend Wilhelm Hoffmann seemed helpless to relieve Gerhard from his despondence. And as his desolation deepened, his health began to collapse.

Then serious illness struck. For many weeks Tersteegen lay in his dingy room with no one to care for him. Neglected by the others in the house and dismissed by his own brothers as either insane or beyond their powers of understanding, Gerhard described himself as 'one far away on a great sea when in the stormy skies neither sun nor stars appear'. Yet he was not in total darkness for he could add, 'but my hope is that my Jesus has his hand upon the helm'. Here he was right and as he slowly regained strength these dawning hopes grew brighter. Perhaps he was not 'past mercy's scope' after all. In later years he put into verse some of the thoughts that encouraged him at that time:

> God calls me yet: at last shall I not heed?
> How long shall I refuse the grace I need?
> God and my soul how oft have I betrayed!
> He draws me still: rise, heart, be not afraid.

When he was well enough to leave his room once more, he undertook a journey to the nearby town of Duisburg, possibly in an attempt to sell his work. His route lay through a wood and as he passed through he was suddenly taken violently ill once more. 'Perhaps I am dying,' he thought in desperation. Falling to the ground he begged God to remove the intense pain and give him time to prepare for eternity. Quite suddenly the pain eased. His cry was heard. There and then Gerhard cast himself on the mercy of God, imploring him to forgive his sins and accept his soul for Christ's sake. He realized at last that no good works of his could earn the favour of God, nor did God set standards he must reach before he could merit salvation.

The next day, back in his room once more, Tersteegen was sitting on his bed when quite unexpectedly his soul was flooded with love to Christ. It was as though a light had been turned on in his innermost being. That spring morning in 1724 was one he would never forget. Already he had begun to express his thoughts in verse and now he wrote words that conveyed his astonishment at knowing at last that his sins were forgiven:

Stars in God's sky

To heart and soul how sweet thou art,
   O great High Priest of God!
My heart brought nigh to God's own heart
   by thy most precious blood.

No more my countless sins shall rise
   to fill me with dismay —
that precious blood before his eyes,
   has put them all away.

Is all a dream? Thou canst not lie;
   thy Spirit and thy blood
proclaim to sinners such as I
   the boundless love of God.

They tell thy love so deep, so free,
   they tell the Father's heart —
not what I am, or I must be,
   they tell me what thou art.

It happened to be the Thursday of Easter week, 1724, and as Tersteegen thought of the sacrifice of Calvary, the Saviour's redeeming work took on new dimensions for the young German. Using his own blood as his ink, he wrote burning words of self-dedication and thanksgiving:

My Jesus, I own myself to be yours; my only Saviour and Bridegroom, Christ Jesus, I am yours, wholly and eternally... From this evening to all eternity, your will not mine be done. Command and rule and reign over me. I yield myself up without reserve and I promise, with your help and power, rather to give up the last drop of this my blood, than knowingly or willingly in my heart or in my life, to be untrue or disobedient to you.

No one rejoiced more in Tersteegen's new-found liberty in Christ than his friend Wilhelm Hoffmann. A wise man, he could see an intrinsic danger for the new convert in his long hours spent alone. Despite Gerhard's love of solitude, he needed companionship, and it was Hoffmann who suggested that Heinrich Sommers, a young and earnest Christian, should join him in his business of ribbon or band weaving. Sommers would also share the house Tersteegen had now purchased in the centre of Mülheim.[1] It was an experiment that lasted for the next forty-four years when death eventually parted the friends. Together they toiled all day, still giving as much as possible from their business enterprises for the relief of the poor and suffering. But this time Gerhard had a new motivation for all his actions: to please Christ and to feel his presence near.

Against all previous expectations, Tersteegen, now twenty-seven years of age, was about to embark on a life of extraordinary usefulness and influence for the kingdom of God, not only among his own countrymen but far down the generations of the Christian church. This he accomplished initially by the poems he wrote. His first book of poems, published in 1729, just five years after his experience in the woods, bore a title which can be translated *Spiritual Flower Garden for Ardent Souls.*[2] Some of the items were written while he was still searching for spiritual answers, but others expressed in words of exquisite beauty the thoughts and aspirations that filled his mind now that he was freed from the burden of his former state.

A number of these poems have been translated into English, and some have become hymns. With an excellent knowledge of German and a heart in tune with his, Frances Bevan, a gifted English poet born in 1827, gave the Christian public the opportunity to sing some of Tersteegen's finest hymns. Catherine Winkworth, another German scholar also born in 1827, and Samuel Jackson (1761-1847), a prominent Methodist leader, added to the collection available in English. Perhaps the best-known translator of all was John Wesley himself who gave us one of Tersteegen's greatest hymns, still to be found in most modern hymn-books:

> Thou hidden love of God, whose height,
>   whose depth unfathomed, no man knows;
> I see from far thy beauteous light,
>   And inly sigh for thy repose;
> my heart is pained, nor can it be
> at rest till it finds rest in thee.

Overwhelmed with gladness at the unexpected mercy of God shown to him, Tersteegen could hardly find words to express his present longing to serve his God. Such words have continued to express the desires of Christians ever since.

> Each moment draw from earth away
>   my heart, that lowly waits thy call;
> speak to my inmost soul and say,
>   'I am thy love, thy God, thy all!'
> To feel thy power, to hear thy voice,
> to taste thy love, be all my choice.

Love and gratitude to God and the desire to serve others now became a driving force for the remainder of Tersteegen's life. Not long after his conversion there was a further widespread awakening in the area where he lived, centred largely on Mülheim itself. Hoffmann's preaching had been the instrument God used to stir up a deep spiritual concern among the people. Unable to deal with all the calls on his time and strength, Hoffmann persuaded Tersteegen to assist him in the preaching. Scarcely had Tersteegen begun to do so than it became clear that God had given him a remarkable gift as a preacher. Crowds flocked from outlying districts to hear him and to join in the prayer meetings. The deep sense of reverence — a fruit of the revival — is expressed in another hymn translated by John Wesley:

Lo! God is here! Let us adore,
and own how dreadful is this place!
Let all within us feel his power
and silent bow before his face;
who know his power, his grace who prove,
serve him with fear, with reverence love.

In addition to his preaching gifts, it became clear that Gerhard's concern for others had made him a wise and able counsellor. He became known as a *Seelenführer* — a guide of souls. Not only did he care for the souls of the people, but in days when the cost of medical assistance was often beyond the reach of the poor, he began to dispense advice and simple medicines. Much of his knowledge was derived from the study of the properties of plants and many of his remedies proved remarkably effective. Asking no fee for his home-made pills and powders, Tersteegen soon found his home besieged throughout the day by the needy men and women of Mülheim and the surrounding area. And always he tried to discern those problems which, like many of his own in former days, sprang from distress of conscience. Such loss of privacy represented considerable self-sacrifice for one whose supreme delight was to spend hours alone in communion with God. Well could he write:

Across the will of nature
leads on the path of God;
not where the flesh delighteth
the feet of Jesus trod.

As the months passed, it became clear that Tersteegen and his friend Heinrich Sommers could no longer combine their services for the people with their work as ribbon weavers. In 1728 they made the decision to give themselves wholly to the spiritual and physical needs of the community. By this time Tersteegen was also employed in further literary work. Over seven hundred poems, together with numerous letters, sermons and biographical accounts of noble Christian men and women, have survived from the pen of this godly man.

And still the crowds thronged Tersteegen's home. Visitors called upon him from many European countries, including Britain. The demands on his time became even greater as he responded to requests to travel far beyond his own boundaries. An annual visit to Holland was undertaken at the persistence of some of his Dutch friends. 'Had I twelve or thirteen years ago foreseen all the roads I would have to travel, I should have rather chosen to die, for I should have thought them hurtful to my soul,' Tersteegen once remarked. On the contrary, he learnt to pray as he went along and now discovered a divine traveller who drew near as he journeyed and whose companionship became precious to him.

A further development came in Tersteegen's life when a merchant by the name of Otterbeck offered to give him the use of his spacious home and garden as a 'Home for Pilgrims'. Like Howell Harris's community in Trevecca, Wales, and at much the same time, this would provide a home for those Christians who wished to live a communal life, while continuing to earn their own support by maintaining their trades. It had adequate accommodation for eight people, each with separate rooms; a prayer-bell would summon all the residents to a time of daily corporate worship.

In 1746 Tersteegen's trusted friend Wilhelm Hoffmann died after a long and painful illness. Gerhard, who had cared for him until the end, greatly missed him. When he discovered that Hoffman had bequeathed his house to be used as another 'Home for Pilgrims', Tersteegen was able to expand this work still further. Before long, two or three more such communities were formed and Tersteegen was fully occupied in paying regular visits to these Homes for Pilgrims, ministering to the spiritual needs of the people.

Tersteegen has sometimes been called a mystic. But he was not a mystic in the classic sense of the word: his was a biblical mysticism which has characterized many of the noblest believers down through the centuries — a 'mysticism' that finds delight in a close communion with Christ and expresses itself in words such as these:

Sweet is the vision of thy face,
and kindness o'er thy lips is shed;
lovely thou art and full of grace,
and glory beams around thy head.

Thy sufferings I embrace with thee,
thy poverty and shameful cross;
the pleasures of the world I flee,
and count its treasures worthless dross.

For many years Tersteegen had suffered from poor health. Possibly his early asceticism had broken his constitution, as it did for George Whitefield. But now when he was weak and ill, instead of lying alone in a gloomy room, thirsty and in pain as he had done in his early days, Tersteegen was surrounded by those who loved and cared for him. And with such attention his years were prolonged. In April 1769, however, when he was seventy-one, the end came. Suffering severely with a lung disorder, he was obliged to remain seated in his chair night and day. For all who came to visit him — and there were many — he had a word of encouragement or challenge. 'O sister, the way is a good way,' he said to one. 'Follow the Lamb with cheerfulness wherever he leads you.' 'May the great High Priest, Jesus, bless you with love and peace in your heart,' he said to another. As death approached, Tersteegen slept much but in his waking moments was heard to whisper constantly, 'O Jesus! O beloved Jesus!' 'Then,' wrote one, 'it was as if the kiss of heavenly love released the imprisoned spirit.' The poet had entered into a long-anticipated joy. At last he could have unbroken communion with the Saviour:

> The years of longing over,
>   do we behold your face;
> we seek no more than you have given,
>   we ask no vision fair,
> your precious blood has opened heaven,
>   and we have found you there.

Notes

1. This building is now used as a museum, displaying Tersteegen's effects and many of his surviving papers, some only recently discovered.
2. Republished seven times in Tersteegen's lifetime, each edition containing additional items, more than 700 in all.

Isabella Graham

trained in Christ's school

*Born in Lanarkshire, Scotland, in 1742,
the same year that revival broke out in Cambuslang
under George Whitefield, Isabella Graham's life
holds much of interest still. Often suffering and
learning some hard lessons, she became eminently
useful in helping others, particularly those in need
following two devastating epidemics of Yellow Fever
in New York in the late eighteenth and
early nineteenth centuries.*

Isabella Graham
(1742-1814)

trained in Christ's school

Isabella Graham faced a dire predicament. Her husband John had died unexpectedly of a tropical fever, leaving her alone with her three small daughters, the eldest only five years of age, and with a fourth child expected shortly. Far from home and with few financial resources to her name, the young mother scarcely knew what to do.

Born in Lanarkshire, Scotland, in 1742, Isabella came from a farming family. While she was still young they had moved to Paisley and it was here that the girl grew up, coming under the influence and preaching of John Witherspoon, who was later to become principal of Princeton College, New Jersey, USA. Like many who have had the privilege of being taught the truths of God from an early age, Isabella could not recollect the time when those truths were not her own inward and personal convictions. Even as a young child she would wander in the woods near her home and pour out her troubles and anxieties to God in prayer. When she was seventeen Isabella was accepted as a communicant member of Dr Witherspoon's congregation.

It was in Paisley that she first met John Graham, a young doctor whose future career seemed bright with possibilities. When Isabella was twenty-three they married and a year or two later John accepted a commission as army doctor to a regiment then based in Canada. In days when a voyage across the Atlantic was fraught with hazards, Isabella and John's transfer to Montreal meant that they had little prospect of seeing Scotland again for many years.

After spending a few months in Montreal, John Graham was informed that he was to be stationed at the army barracks at Fort Niagara on Lake Ontario. And here during the next four years their three daughters, Jessica, Joanna and Isabella, were born. Although these were happy years for the family, the army base was isolated from the rest of the community with no provision made for any Christian ministry. Isabella would later acknowledge that even though she spent time on a Sunday reading her Bible and in prayer, the loss was a serious one and the years barren spiritually.

As tension rose between Britain and her American colonies in 1773, John Graham's regiment received orders from the British government to move to the island of Antigua. But by this time John was growing tired of the strictures of army life, and found his new environment, with its long sandy beaches fringed by palm trees, highly attractive. He decided to sell his commission, buy land on that sun-drenched island, and perhaps bring his parents and other members of his family still in Scotland to join him and his wife Isabella there. Before she had been on the island for long, Isabella met some Antiguan Methodists whose zeal and piety strengthened and renewed her own spirit. John too, whose religion had been little more than formal, began to show a concern for spiritual things.

Only a year later, after just nine years of marriage, their prospects were shattered as John's life was unexpectedly cut short. He had succumbed to a virulent tropical fever against which he seemed to have little resistance. Despite the fact that his illness had not appeared serious at first, John Graham had a premonition that he would not live and had shared his fears with Isabella. His last words suggested that in those final days of life John had at last found an anchor for his soul and confidence in Christ to pardon his past and carry him through death.

All Isabella's material hopes, joys and plans had turned to dust in a few short days. But in her need she turned back to the God in whom she had trusted from early years for comfort and guidance. Yet understandably the shock of John's death brought on a deep depression, confusing and clouding her mind. As the day for her confinement drew ever closer Isabella became convinced that she would not survive childbirth.

Her pressing anxiety therefore was to make some provision for her young family in this desperate circumstance. All she could do was to commit her three little girls and her new baby, so soon to be born, to the care of a friend. But Isabella was wrong — she did not die, for God had purposes for her life, although as yet they had been veiled from her. After the birth of her son, named John after his father, she gradually recovered stability and decided that the only course now open to her was to return home to Scotland with the children.

The sale of John's property in Antigua gave Isabella enough money to cover the cost of the fares on a ship sailing soon to Belfast. Arriving at last in Ireland after a long and stormy voyage, Isabella and her family boarded a smaller vessel to cross the Irish Sea back to Scotland. What she did not know was that this boat was far from seaworthy; it did not even have a compass on board. When a violent storm arose in the night, the chances of survival for the family were slim. For nine hours the vessel was tossed about like a cork, and before long began to disintegrate. Rudder and masts were smashed and carried away, and everything possible thrown overboard to lighten their load. While some crew members and passengers wept, others swore and yet others prayed. All were terrified in the face of imminent death. As Isabella comforted her sobbing girls, with baby John in her arms, she assured her small family that they would soon join their father once more in a better world.

Then with a grinding crunch and ear-splitting crash the ship hit a rock not far from Ayr on the west coast of Scotland. 'Is there any peace here?' cried one dismayed passenger as he looked into Isabella's cabin and saw her calm-looking face. Even though the hold was rapidly filling with water, she and the unknown fellow passenger read together words from Psalm 107: 'He maketh the storm a calm and stilleth the waves thereof' (AV). No sooner had they read these words than they felt the stricken vessel move slightly as the rising tide began to lift it off the rock. Amazingly, the ship was able to list to shore and here it became grounded on a sandbank. Locals soon mounted a rescue operation as the frightened passengers were taken to safety. For Isabella the entire experience was a token that the God in whom she had placed her trust would care for her and for her fatherless children.

The family had not been long on dry ground before Isabella recognized an acquaintance from earlier years among the kindly faces of the people of Ayr who had gathered on the shore. Explaining her situation, she gratefully accepted help to travel on to Paisley where she hoped to be reunited with the family she had not seen for six years. However, a further shock awaited Isabella. Her mother had died in the interval and although she found her father alive, he was living in abject poverty following the death of his wife and the loss of all his money.

Bravely Isabella undertook to care for him in his declining years. With the small income which she earned from some teaching work, she ran his home and cared for her children. Gone were all the luxuries to which she and her husband John had grown accustomed. Attractive clothes for her girls were a thing of the past as the family now lived with utmost frugality. Their diet was basic: potatoes for dinner, and nothing but porridge for both breakfast and supper. Yet Isabella was happy; God had provided a home for her and in these reduced circumstances she was content. Above all, she experienced renewed spiritual joys which she had all but lost when everything had been well outwardly. Unknown to her at the time, these experiences were a preparation for a surprising degree of usefulness in the future and would prove a vital part of her training for that task.

At last in 1780, after the death of her father and six years after John's death, the educational needs of the girls became an important factor. Isabella decided to move to Edinburgh where she planned to open a boarding school for girls, one that her own three could attend, so mixing with others of their own age. But at this point Isabella made a serious mistake as she afterwards acknowledged with deep regret. In order to run such a school she would have neither time nor means to care adequately for her young son, John, now just six years of age. What could she do with him? The decision she made was to place him in the care of a friend who would oversee the boy's education. But John needed his mother, and the friend showed little aptitude for coping with the child. With a lively and mischievous disposition, John soon developed habits and attitudes which would bring much grief to his mother in later years.

Isabella had not been in Edinburgh long before she gained the respect and friendship of Willielma Campbell, better known as Lady Glenorchy. The two women were the same age, both born in the early 1740s, but whereas Isabella had experienced days of severe financial hardship, her new friend had a considerable estate at her disposal. Like Isabella, Willielma had also lost her husband not long after her marriage, but this placed her in a position to use all her resources in the service of Christ. She financed the building of a number of new chapels both in Scotland and England, supported the Christian ministry whenever she had opportunity, and gave generously towards the education of many who would otherwise have had no such opportunities. Although Willielma frequently helped Isabella when times were hard, the friendship was mutual for she depended on Isabella's love and understanding. More than this, Isabella was able to give assistance in the many charitable projects which Willielma had undertaken, particularly when her friend was too ill to meet some commitment herself. Willielma's great respect for Isabella was expressed in her known request that if her friend were within twenty miles of her when she was dying she would come and stay with her to the end.

In 1786 it seemed certain that Willielma had not much longer to live and Isabella was able to fulfil this wish and to watch by her during those last days. With Willielma's death at the early age of forty-five, there now seemed little to keep Isabella in Scotland. Her friend had died, the education of her three daughters was almost complete, and with few ties left in Scotland, Isabella decided to emigrate, returning to New York where she had spent some months previously with her husband, John. Together with her three daughters, Jessica, Joanna and her own namesake, young Isabella, she undertook the hazardous voyage across the Atlantic once again in 1789. Never again would she visit her own Scottish shores.

Isabella's fifteen-year-old son John remained behind in Scotland, ostensibly to complete his education. Perhaps the boy had now become too difficult for his mother to handle. Wild and adventurous, he had also proved impossible for his guardians to manage and at his insistence they allowed the youth to join the merchant navy. Meanwhile Isabella once more opened a school for girls, this time in New York, with her pupils increasing from five to fifty within the first month.

Perhaps one of the most interesting and instructive aspects of Isabella Graham's life lies in her relationship with her four children; her earnest prayers and desires for them, and even her remorse at wrong decisions made concerning them. Certainly, it would seem that she made a serious mistake with her son, but there can be few parents who do not look back with some measure of regret on the circumstances and unwise choices they may have made during the upbringing of their children. Isabella's joy when each of her girls responded personally to the gospel of Christ was deep and heartfelt:

> Glory! Glory! Glory! To the hearer of prayer. I have cast my fatherless children on the Lord, and he has begun to make good my confidence. One thing, only one thing have I asked for them... I seek for my four children and for myself first of all 'the kingdom of God'.

For more than two years Isabella received no word at all about what had happened to her son. But things had not been going well for John. He had only been at sea a short time before the ship in which he was sailing was wrecked near the coast of Holland. Taken ashore in Rotterdam, John was destitute and alone with no one to whom to turn. At last, after two years, a friend of Isabella's in Rotterdam discovered the youth living in desperate circumstances and realized with horror that he was Isabella's son. This friend cared for him, clothed him and eventually paid for his passage to New York where he was reunited with his family in 1791, two years after Isabella had left Scotland.

Yet John still could not settle down. His urge to return to the sea was intense, and at last Isabella could see that she must let him go. Her anguish over him was great: 'This day my only son left me in bitter wringings of heart; he is launched again on the ocean — God's ocean. The Lord saved him from shipwreck, brought him to my home… He has been with me but a short time and ill have I improved it — now he is gone from my sight and my heart bursts with tumultuous grief.'

Isabella had learnt from long experience where to take her griefs and anxieties, and her prayer for John was heartfelt:

Lord have mercy on the widow's son — the only son of his mother. I ask nothing in all this world for him: I repeat my petition, save his soul alive, give him salvation from sin. It is not the danger from the seas that distresses me … it is not the dread of never seeing him again in this world. It is because I cannot discern the new birth nor its fruits, but every symptom of captivity to Satan, the world and self will. O Lord, many wonders hast thou shown me; call, convert, regenerate and establish a sailor in the faith. Lord, all things are possible with thee. I wait for thy salvation.

Three more years were to pass before Isabella heard again from John. Day by day she watched, waited and prayed, but still received no news. At last a long-looked-for letter came, sent from the West Indies. It told of the many disasters that had befallen him. First the ship on which he was serving was boarded by a press-gang, and although the young man was not coerced into military service, he was robbed of all his possessions. The captain of the ship had treated him badly, and as a result John had been seriously ill. Twice he had been taken prisoner, but now, after his second release, he was writing to say that he planned to sail back to Europe. In his letter John, who was twenty years of age at the time, reflected on the course of his life and expressed the hope that he would learn by his experiences. But it was the last Isabella would ever hear from her son.

Like any Christian mother, Isabella clung to that single strand of hope from this last letter, and prayed that John might indeed have reflected on his life and have been saved by God's grace at the last. She deeply regretted that she had ever allowed him to leave her at so young an age, and throughout the remainder of her life continued to express her regrets over this as well as her continued hopes and longings for 'my prodigal's return' to the Father's house.

Nor was the uncertainty and increasing fears over John the only trial that Isabella faced at this time. Her eldest daughter, Jessica, still only twenty-six years of age, became seriously ill. Although the young woman had suffered indifferent health for some time, her death in 1795 was a severe loss to her mother who described her as 'my companion, my affectionate child'. An earnest Christian, gentle and loving by nature, Jessica faced the approach of death courageously.

'I wish you joy, my darling,' said Isabella as she knew for certain that Jessica was dying. The mother's initial triumph over her grief was a remarkable testimony to the strength of her faith. But this did not cancel out the waves of human sorrow that almost overwhelmed her as she began to plumb the depths of her bereavement. In some respects this very natural grief makes Isabella's faith appear the more attractive:

Why, O why is my spirit still depressed? Father forgive! Jesus wept; I weep but acquiesce. This day two months ago the Lord delivered my Jessie from a body of sin and death; finished the good work he had begun and carried her triumphant through the valley of the shadow of death... I did rejoice, I do rejoice, but O Lord, you know my frame ... my soul feels a want. O fill it up with more of your presence.

Not long after these family sorrows Isabella Graham began that significant aspect of Christian service on which most biographical accounts of her life concentrate as the major theme of their narrative. It was a work for which God had long been preparing her through the experiences she herself had known. In 1798 a widespread epidemic of Yellow Fever had broken out in New York. Unaware that this killer-disease was spread through mosquito bites, little precaution was taken to eradicate the pests by destroying their habitats. Among the symptoms of this illness were a soaring fever, backache, headache, sickness and the characteristic yellowing of the skin which gave the condition its name. Death would normally follow within a week of the illness first striking. Men working on road or other construction projects were particularly vulnerable and throughout New York women with young children were left destitute by the death of their husbands. Such a plight was one for which Isabella had a natural sympathy, for she had trodden that same lonely path herself.

The Widows' Society, as it was called, had been founded the previous year, but it was Isabella's enthusiasm and service as the director of this society for the next ten years of her life that gave it both impetus and widespread support. All her energies were now channelled into bringing relief to poverty-stricken families and, more than this, to comfort those who grieved with those same consolations that had sustained her in her need. 'Jesus himself was a Man of Sorrows,' she wrote to one young mother, 'his face marred with grief. He, even he, was made perfect through suffering ... O for faith in the wisdom and the love of God, and for patience to endure to the end.'

So contagious was the Yellow Fever that few doctors would attend the dying, and many women had to place their own dead into the coffin delivered to the house. They had no one to assist them, nor any to attend the funeral. Eleven doctors who had been prepared to give help wherever they could had themselves died in the epidemic. Some people fled the city, only to find their predicament yet worse as they died alone with no family to care. These sorrows touched Isabella deeply and she did all in her power to help those who were suffering and to collect donations for their relief.

As the epidemic abated, it came as a shock to Isabella to discover that even so fearful an event seemed to leave the people untouched spiritually. Most shrugged their shoulders and took the attitude that such things were best forgotten, and in any case unlikely to happen again. But they were wrong. A mere two years later a further devastating epidemic broke out in New York, leaving few households untouched by the death of a husband, wife or child. Isabella's work soon stretched beyond raising financial help for widows and orphans. Women needed work so that they could support themselves; their children needed educational facilities. In 1804, even though Isabella was now sixty-two years of age and far from strong herself, she supervised the opening of a school for such children and soon afterwards founded an orphanage for the many who had lost both parents in the Yellow Fever epidemics. Before long, the extent of her concerns stretched to the women's prisons and to the desperate condition of slaves who became sick and were therefore useless to their owners.

Living with one or other of her married daughters in turn, Isabella cared for the spiritual life of her grandchildren even as she had watched over her own three daughters. But by 1812 it became clear that the life of this noble and self-denying woman was drawing to a close. At seventy years of age she found that she no longer had the strength to visit the distressed as she had done for so long. But she did not fret against her limitations; instead she actively prepared her mind and spirit for that time when her God would call her to himself. She read much, finding the writings of William Romaine, John Newton and John Owen of particular encouragement to her spirit.

In days of illness and failing strength it is often hard to read, pray and draw strength from God to face that 'last enemy' — death itself. More than this, Satan often takes advantage of our weakness and assails the believer with doubts, fears and reminders of past sins. Isabella knew this, having sat with so many as they were dying. And she decided to anticipate such an eventuality by preparing what she called her *Book of Provisions against the Crossing of Jordan.* A grand title maybe, but in essence this was a collection of verses of hymns, passages of Scripture and extracts from books she had read which she felt would help her in that last hour of need. Many of the hymns she learnt by heart so that when she was unable to sleep she could sing her 'songs in the night'. And when she was no longer able to read to herself from her *Book of Provisions,* she would ask anyone who came to her bedside to read to her out of her book. Hymns referring to the power of Jesus Christ to answer all the accusations of Satan on behalf of his people were timely in Isabella Graham's experience. She found special consolation from John Newton's words:

Let us love and sing and wonder:
   let us praise the Saviour's name!
He has hushed the law's loud thunder;
   he has quenched Mount Sinai's flame;
he has washed us with his blood;
   he has brought us nigh to God.

And the end was triumphant. As her distressed family stood around, Isabella was able to say, 'My dear children, I have no more doubt about going to my Saviour than if I were already in his arms; my guilt is all transferred; he has cancelled all I owed. Yet I could weep for sins against so good a God.' All her life she had carried with her a sense of her failures and sins, yet now at the last she had the peaceful confidence that those things to which Satan could point had been pardoned through Christ. Nothing now remained but for the Saviour to call her home. Those who watched over her noticed the settled peace that marked her features in the last hours of her life and on 27 July 1814 she was taken at last to a land where sin, sorrow and regret are gone for ever.

Hugh Bourne

and the birth of Primitive Methodism

Hugh Bourne, a shy farmer's son who struggled for twenty years before finding assurance of God's favour, was used powerfully in a revival that began in the Potteries in Staffordshire during the early years of the nineteenth century. This unusual work of God would result in the creation of the country-wide Primitive Methodist movement.

Hugh Bourne
(1772-1852)

and the birth of Primitive Methodism

Joseph Bourne was drunk again. Three-year-old Hugh could hear his father's unsteady footsteps returning to his isolated farmstead, and he cowered closer to his mother. It had not always been like this. After inheriting a thriving pottery business from his own father, Joseph, together with his wife Ellen, had left the Potteries in Staffordshire and travelled up to Greenock in Scotland, where he began to sell his pottery ware. At first trade flourished, but at the same time Joseph began to drink heavily. When the business faltered the young couple decided to return with their children to their former home Ford Hay Farm, not far from Milton, just north-east of Stoke-on-Trent.

Not many months later their third son, Hugh, was born on 3 April 1772. As the child grew, he began to fear his father, who was by now displaying drunken outbursts of temper and unpredictable behaviour. Quiet by nature, Hugh found in his mother Ellen an anchor and refuge for his childhood years.

Later he would write of her, 'My mother was a woman of such prudence, management, industry and economy that could not be surpassed, if equalled.' Religious and upright, she taught young Hugh to read as she sat at her spinning wheel. She taught him the Ten Commandments, and implanted in her son concepts of God, and his glory and power, which shaped the boy's thinking throughout his life. She also instilled into her child a rigid code of conduct. Sabbath-keeping was strictly inculcated; lying, petty theft and many childish failings were severely reprimanded.

Eight children were born to Joseph and Ellen, and times were often hard at Ford Hay Farm as they struggled to provide for a growing family. In addition to cultivating the land, Joseph Bourne ventured into the timber trade and learnt the skills of a wheelwright. The farm lay well off the beaten track and few visitors made their way up to the isolated homestead. Shy to a fault, Hugh grew up awkward and ill at ease in company, a trait that would follow him throughout adult life, but one he struggled against and overcame to a remarkable degree.

Conscientious and sincere though he was, young Hugh Bourne trod a long and daunting path before he found any assurance of forgiveness of sins through the merits and death of Christ. From the age of seven the child had begun to read his Bible seriously and to realize that he fell far short of God's standards. Perhaps hell would open its gates at any moment and take him in, he thought apprehensively. His fears increased sharply after an incident, trivial enough it may seem, but one that had long-lasting consequences for Hugh.

A kindly neighbouring farmer used to supply coal for the Bourne family, leaving it at the bottom of their field, near a small stream. The older children in the family would then fling a plank of wood across the stream, fill a basket with coal and walk back carefully along the plank, carrying the coal. Hugh wanted to try the feat but he was only ten. Doubtless, thought his siblings, he would fall into the stream together with his basket of coal. At last he persuaded them to let him try. But before his attempt Hugh made a promise to God. If God would help him to manage the crossing, he would ensure that all his family worshipped God. Succeeding in his balancing act to the amazed congratulations of all, Hugh tried to keep his promise, but inevitably failed. This one incident preyed on his mind night and day. Although unintentionally, he felt he had lied to God. He had broken his word. Now surely hell must be his portion.

If only there had been someone to point the troubled child to the mercy and forgiveness of God. But there was no one. His mother's belief that the road to salvation lay in attaining her high ethical standards left him in despair. Each night as he went to bed he feared to fall asleep, lest he awoke in hell. For the next twenty years, from the age of seven until twenty-seven, Hugh Bourne remained in this state, finding neither spiritual peace nor anyone who could help him and show him one who could save him from his sins.

With a mixture of pride and good intentions, Joseph Bourne thought that this serious-minded son of his ought to be 'a parson' and was therefore willing that the boy should have an education. With a voracious love of learning, Hugh gave himself diligently to his studies and received a firm grounding in the basics of numeracy and the arts. But Joseph's well-meaning purposes soon came to an end. He needed the boy on the farm, and Hugh was taken from school to learn instead the skills of a wheelwright and the running of a timber business. But each night, long after the rest of the family slept, Hugh's candle was still burning as he tried to continue his education on his own.

Ill-tempered and impatient, his father was no easy task-master and Hugh was relieved when he was sent instead to his uncle's home to learn the skills of engineering involved with the craft of a millwright. And still the inner spiritual turmoil continued. Occasionally he heard Methodist preachers, but now he compared his own high standards of morality learnt from his mother with the faults he observed in the lives of some Methodists and dismissed the message they were preaching.

At last in 1799, when Hugh Bourne was twenty-seven, God's moment of deliverance for this young man dawned. He had always read any religious book that he could obtain with urgent concern, but nothing seemed to answer his deep fears and overwhelming sense of failure before a holy God — until at last, by a circuitous route, one important book came his way. A chunky tome, the book had been lent to his mother, but it had not taken Hugh long to find it and to start to read it. Composed of a wide variety of sermons and treatises, it included the work of the Puritans, Richard Baxter and Joseph Alleine. Also bound up in the same volume was a sermon by John Wesley. Hugh read it avidly and as he did so his aversion to the Methodists and many of his presuppositions concerning them were swept away. Later he wrote that this one book gave him 'more light and information than any book I had ever read…' Now prepared to consider Methodist writings, Hugh gladly received copies of the *Methodist Magazine* from a friend. But when he read John Fletcher of Madeley's *Letters on the Spiritual Manifestation of the Son of God,* which had been published in the 1793 issue, Hugh Bourne's tortured mind was flooded with light, understanding and joy. Writing of this in later years Hugh could say:

One Sunday morning in my father's house, as I was reading in Mr Fletcher's letters on the spiritual manifestation of the Son of God … Christ manifested himself to me, and I was born again in an instant! Yea, passed from death unto life. The naughty was taken out of my heart, and the good put in. In an instant I had power over sin which I had not had before; and I was filled with joy, and love, and glory which made full amends for twenty years of suffering. The Bible looked new; creation looked new; and I felt a love for all mankind; and my desire was that friends and enemies, and all the world, if possible, might be saved.

Hugh then faced a fresh dilemma. Normally he worshipped at his local parish church, but now he could see that it lacked that spiritual vitality which had brought life and pardon to his own soul. Yet to leave and to join the Methodists was a hard step indeed. The young convert earnestly prayed to God for direction, but the method God used was far different from anything Hugh could have imagined.

Old Farmer Birchenough had been watching the young man with interest and concern. 'Will you not join me at a Methodist love-feast at Burslem?' he enquired not long after Bourne's conversion. These love-feasts were a regular part of the life of the early Methodists and included a time of mutual fellowship and sharing of spiritual experience. Having read much in the *Methodist Magazine* about the love-feasts, Hugh was anxious to experience one for himself and so readily consented to his friend's proposal. As he entered the Burslem Methodist chapel where the love-feast was to be held, he discovered he would need a ticket in order to attend. Without any further enquiries, the steward in charge accordingly issued Bourne with a ticket, writing his name on it. What Hugh did not realize was that this ticket made him a *de facto* member of the Burslem Methodist Society. But by the end of the love-feast he had experienced such sweetness and joy in the company of other believers that when he discovered that he had inadvertently become a member of the society, he was able to recognize God's hand in it. From then on he changed his allegiance from the parish church to the Methodists, joining the society which met at Ridgeway, a small rural community not far from Bemersley, where his family now lived. Before long his mother Ellen joined him as God delivered her from a trust in her own righteousness, leading her into a humble dependence on Christ. It is not hard to imagine Hugh's joy over this, and particularly when one of his brothers, James, was also converted.

The passion of Hugh's new-found spiritual freedom was, as he had expressed it, 'that friends and enemies, and all the world, if possible, might be saved'. Painfully shy though he was, this became the goal of his existence as a Christian. But with such a temperament, how could he share his experience? One solution which he decided upon was to write out an account of his conversion and give it to his friends and acquaintances to read.

When his work as a timber merchant took him to a colliery at Harriseahead, north-east of Kidsgrove, Hugh was dismayed. The thought of such a rough and godless area made him tremble. How could he, so young a believer, stand fast

Hugh Bourne

in that environment? But this very situation was inextricably linked with God's purposes for the young man and indeed, for a future, though yet unknown, work of God. As he had planned, Hugh decided to give a copy of his conversion experience to the local blacksmith, Thomas Maxfield. Like all smithies, Maxfield's workshop was a place where the men would regularly gather and exchange all the gossip of the day.

One day Daniel Shubotham came into the smithy — he had already heard of the piety of Bourne, who was in fact a second cousin of his. With his customary oaths, Shubotham — a man with an infamous reputation as a waster turned poacher, turned boxer and perpetrator of all manner of petty crime — began cursing Hugh Bourne. But Thomas Maxfield, the blacksmith, who had read Bourne's written experiences, interrupted. 'Ay, lad,' he said, 'but he is a safe [saved] mon.' Daniel's reaction was astonishing: 'Then I will be a safe mon, for I'll go and join him.' And he did.

Shy as he was, such an opportunity gave Hugh Bourne an unexpected freedom of speech, and on Christmas Day 1800, just six months after he himself had been converted, he 'preached' his first sermon to a one-man congregation. He entreated Daniel with all the urgency he knew to turn from his sins and flee to Jesus Christ for mercy before hell swallowed him up for ever. Discouraged at what appeared the failure of his attempts, Bourne returned to his home, feeling he had done little good. But unknown to him his cousin had been powerfully converted. When Daniel reached his house, he discovered his old companions awaiting him ready for a game of cards. To their amazement Daniel read a passage of the Bible to them instead and urged them all to come to heaven with him, but insisted he would not accompany them to hell. One by one they left the house, saying that Hugh Bourne had driven Daniel mad. But Shubotham had never been more sane. Not surprisingly, such a conversion was the talk of the whole area, and this marked the beginning of an astonishing work of God, spreading outwards from the Staffordshire collieries — a work which would eventually need a new name, that of Primitive Methodism.

Before long another miner, Matthias Bailey, was converted, and together the three enjoyed remarkable Christian fellowship. Described as 'famous talkers for the Lord', these men were irrepressible. Wherever they went they spoke to all of their need of salvation and gradually the nucleus of new believers was enlarged and strengthened.

However, one thing was missing. There were no prayer meetings, nor had Bourne, Shubotham or Bailey ever prayed aloud before. Realizing their lack, they decided to hold a meeting for prayer hoping they could perhaps find some Methodist to lead it for them. But no one seemed available. Anxiously these three labouring men then searched through a prayer book looking for some suitable prayer that would express their desires for the conversion of souls — but without success.

At last they realized that they had no alternative but to try to pray aloud together. Matthias Bailey started and was so helped in his petitions that Hugh Bourne felt he could never pray. But he did; and Matthias in turn was astonished at the liberty given to his friend. Describing the occasion later, Hugh scarcely had words to tell of the assistance of the Spirit of God that he had experienced. 'The instant I began heaven opened in my soul and my course throughout was glorious — grace and glory rested upon me all the time I prayed.'

Having tasted the blessings of open prayer, a regular gathering was established, and before long so many wished to attend and to take part that no alternative remained other than for all to pray aloud at once — and very noisy these prayer meetings were. It is said that the sound of prayer could be heard a mile and a half away. Those who were timid could pray without fear, for we read that 'anyone who could distinguish his or her own voice must have had a pretty good ear'. Yet they were controlled too. Because these men had to be up early for work, the meetings were not permitted to go on for more than an hour or an hour and a quarter at the most. So anxious were they to utilize every possible moment for prayer that they even established 'walking prayer meetings' as they walked to and from work each day. On occasions the spirit of prayer was with them to such a degree that they were reluctant to stop praying. After one such prayer meeting Daniel Shubotham made a surprising suggestion: 'One day,' he said, 'you shall have a whole day of prayer on Mow Cop' — a craggy mountain that rose one thousand feet above the village of Harriseahead. He spoke truer than he knew.

Mow Cop

In answer to these urgent prayers the God of heaven poured out his blessing on this community. The work spread and the whole district was gradually transformed by the changed lives of new converts. In 1801, just two years after his own conversion, Hugh Bourne was prevailed upon, although unwillingly, to preach at the home of Joseph Pointon who lived not far from Harriseahead. What if more people came than could be accommodated in Pointon's home? he wondered. And this was indeed the case. So many crowded to hear him that the meeting had to be conducted in a nearby field — a meeting in the open air, as had so often happened in early Methodism. The preacher himself was overcome with nerves to such an alarming extent that he covered up his face with his hands as he spoke — a strange mannerism that would continue with him throughout his life whenever he preached. Exhausted by the effort, Hugh went back into the house while his brother James gave out a hymn with a prayer meeting to follow.

A year or two later a young man of twenty-five, whose influence would be critical to the developing work, was remarkably converted. William Clowes, born at Burslem, Staffordshire, and grandson of the master potter, Josiah Wedgwood, was a natural leader. Although athletic, popular and talented, William had become addicted to drink and had lived a dissolute life until the age of twenty-five when God met and changed him. Concerned about his spiritual state, Clowes had attended a love-feast in Burslem Methodist Society, but under false pretences, using someone else's ticket. Then he panicked when he saw the members sharing a simple meal of cake and water. Perhaps this was a communion service? He did not know. But if it was, then he would be 'eating and drinking damnation to himself', as the Scripture warns all who take part with unbelieving hearts. Terrified that his last hope of salvation was slipping beyond his grasp, the young man was found at the early morning prayer meeting on the following day. 'I cried to One who was mighty to save,' he recorded. During that meeting, as he later testified, 'I felt my bands breaking. In an agony of soul I believed that God *would* save me — then I believed he *was* saving me — then I believed he *had* saved me; and it was so.' William Clowes was a new man in Christ.

It was not long before Hugh Bourne heard of the conversion of this man, so entirely different from himself. Despite his shyness he visited Clowes, and found in him one with whom he was immediately united in love and fellowship. Long into the night they sat talking for they had much to share of God's separate dealings with them. William Clowes was the right man to further this new work of God that was gradually coming to fruition in the Potteries. Bourne soon introduced Clowes to his circle of friends, Daniel Shubotham, Matthias Bailey and many others: potters, miners, farmers — none high up on the social scale of this present world, but men and women transformed by the grace of God and now with a single aim to reach out to the souls of others.

With new impetus following the conversion of Clowes, Hugh Bourne and his friends longed for ways to reach out to a wider section of their community. And just at that time an unusual visitor came to the area, an American known as 'Crazy Dow'. Unconventional and a loner, Lorenzo

Lorenzo Dow

Dow had been powerfully used by God in the Camp Meetings of America. These were remarkable gatherings where preaching and praying went on continuously, day and night, for almost a week, with the people camped out in tents or hastily built log cabins, surrounding the camp fires and pulpits in a great arc.

No privation, suffering or hardship could prevent this intrepid evangelist from striving day and night to win souls for Jesus Christ. Dow would travel from one Camp Meeting to another, often being drenched by rain, sleet or snow and having to sleep rough at night. Never strong, Dow had undermined his health in his evangelistic zeal. Now he was on a short visit to England to recuperate. And in God's purposes, one unlikely place that Dow visited was Harriseahead. Here Hugh Bourne heard him speak at length of God's mighty power displayed at the Camp Meetings. The next day William Clowes walked nine miles to hear Dow preach at Congleton. A new aspiration was born in Hugh's soul that day. Why not have a Camp Meeting on Mow Cop?

First Camp Meeting at Mow Cop

Certainly it seemed a dubious enterprise, but had not Daniel Shubotham promised the people 'a whole day's praying on Mow Cop'? At last plans were finalized for 31 May 1807. On a drizzly Sunday morning a somewhat dispirited group of people climbed Mow Cop — Hugh himself decided not to come, so sure was he that no one would venture up the mountain on such a day. But William Clowes was there, and Hugh afterwards relented and joined them.

A makeshift pulpit was set up, and one of their number began to preach. A few more stragglers joined the group. A time of prayer followed, and as numbers were steadily increasing, a flag was set up to show newcomers where to gather. William Clowes himself climbed into the pulpit and told the ever-increasing crowd of all that God had done for him, making a new man of him by the gospel. And still the numbers multiplied. Before long they needed a second preaching centre so that all could hear the message. Then as yet more struggled up the rocky hillside, swelling the congregations to an estimated three thousand or more, another pulpit was raised; then another. God's Spirit was present amongst these earnest men and women and powerfully owned the preaching. Many were converted and even after a whole day on Mow Cop the crowds only reluctantly dispersed as darkness shrouded the mountain.

So remarkable had been that first Camp Meeting that another was soon planned for 18 July. But this time it was to begin at four o'clock on a Saturday afternoon and to last for two or three days. Tents, lanterns, candles, seating, food: the logistics of such an event were no light undertaking for Hugh Bourne and his friends. Following that Camp Meeting yet another was planned to be held in the village of Norton, just north of Burslem, where Bourne had recently been responsible for the building of a Methodist chapel.

But despite the evident blessing of God on these first Camp Meetings on Mow Cop, not all were happy with such methods. The local preachers of the Burslem Methodist Society expressed their disquiet, warning their members against attending. To disobey the injunctions of the very society where both Bourne and Clowes had received spiritual fellowship and help was hard indeed. Daniel Shubotham could not face it, nor could William Clowes, and both temporarily withdrew their support. But the real trouble arose after the third Camp Meeting, for now even the Methodist Conference, entirely forgetting that its leader, John Wesley, had preached in fields and barns in the early days of Methodism, pronounced against the Camp Meetings. Such gatherings were, said the conference, 'productive of considerable mischief'. Hugh Bourne felt the entire brunt of the opposition falling on him alone. But he knew he must carry on. Throughout the rest of 1807 and during 1808 he continued to organize and finance Camp Meetings, and God continued to save many of those who attended.

Then came a moment that Hugh Bourne had anticipated but resolutely thrust from his mind — he was expelled from the Burslem Methodist Society. No explanation was given, nor any chance provided to defend himself. As Bourne adroitly remarked, he had joined without knowing it, and now had been cast out without prior warning — a hard burden to bear, particularly as he was a trustee of the chapel and had provided generous financial aid.

Perplexed, but unbowed, Hugh held on his way. Each Sunday he could be found walking or riding to distant villages, preaching to any who would listen, and organizing Camp Meetings. Then came a day when he felt a conviction in his soul that God wished him to give up his daily occupation and devote himself wholly to evangelism. How would he manage? He could not tell, but as before he obeyed that inner compunction which he felt sure was from God.

Meanwhile William Clowes, although in personal sympathy with Bourne and the Camp Meetings, remained within the Methodist Society, and was promoted as a lay preacher. But he was not a happy man. At last in 1810, two years after Hugh's expulsion, Clowes once more attended a Camp Meeting. Discipline was draconian and direct. His name was promptly dropped from the membership of the society. Clowes too had effectually been expelled.

But God had not cast out these brave men, and as they fearlessly evangelized wherever they could, their efforts were owned by increasing numbers of conversions. Tunstall, a little north of Burslem, was the home of James Steele who had been a member of the Methodist Society for more than twenty years. He too was excommunicated for his support of Clowes and Bourne. Before long a new society came into being in Tunstall; clearly the old bottles of Methodism could no longer contain

William Clowes

118

the new wine of this fresh movement of the Spirit of God. Like the Wesleys before them, they had been forced out and had no choice other than to form a new grouping — and what better name could they call themselves than *Primitive* Methodists, for they were returning to the ways of the old Methodism which God had so abundantly blessed in the days of the Evangelical Revival of the previous century. On 13 February 1812 a new denomination came into being.

From such small beginnings as a handful of labouring men, touched by the Spirit of God and burning with zeal for the conversion of others, there sprang a mighty work which spread across the entire country. Opposition, persecution, need and deprivation were often the lot of these pioneers, but the rewards were inestimable. Within eighteen years the Primitive Methodists had some 50,000 adherents — not taken from other denominations, but raw converts straight from the world. By the time Hugh Bourne died in 1852, at the age of eighty, the membership of Primitive Methodist chapels, quite apart from those who were adherents, was an amazing 110,000.

Hugh Bourne never married, his shyness proving an obstacle hard to overcome. But as his principal biographer, John Walford, who knew him personally, could write: Hugh Bourne was 'a steady, persevering, inflexible friend to the masses; a wise, watchful and faithful counsellor under many severe trials and bitter persecutions; he lived a blessing to the millions and died a benefactor to the Primitive Methodist Connexion, and his name will live for ever...'

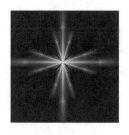

John Gifford

saved from
the hangman's noose

*John Gifford, a Royalist soldier, was condemned
to death in 1648 during the Second Civil War.
Not only did he escape the hangman's noose
but also the just anger of an offended God
as he found forgiveness for his godless life.
He would become John Bunyan's first pastor,
mentor and friend.*

John Gifford
(1602?-1655)

saved from
the hangman's noose

Charles I of England and his Royalist supporters had been soundly defeated by the Parliamentarian armies in the English Civil War which had broken out in 1642. But despite this fact the King had refused to negotiate any satisfactory peace terms with his victorious subjects. In December 1647, even though he was a prisoner in Carisbrooke Castle on the Isle of Wight, Charles had found a way of forming a secret alliance with the Scots: if they would raise an army to fight for him, he would uphold Presbyterianism in his northern kingdom.

Believing he could be trusted to keep his word, the Scottish army had penetrated northern England on behalf of their prisoner-king. Before long, the towns of Carlisle and Berwick had fallen into Royalist hands once more. Heartened by these victories, other defeated Royalist commanders had rallied their troops to join the fray. Fierce fighting broke out in Wales, and while Oliver Cromwell and his Ironsides hastened west to crush that rebellion, news filtered through that Royalists in Kent had also risen to fight the King's cause.

Rumour had it that some twelve thousand armed men from Maidstone, Dover, Canterbury, Deal and other towns in Kent were on the march to London, drums beating, banners waving, clearly spoiling for a fight in support of Charles. Among their leaders was a man, renowned for his corrupt life, drunkenness and gambling habits, who had taken a prominent part in rallying support for the King's cause. His name was John Gifford.

Wasting no time Sir Thomas Fairfax, known as Black Tom, Commander-in-Chief of the New Model Army, rallied his men and galloped off to meet the insurgents. Even though he was suffering severe pain as a result of an earlier war wound, Fairfax was a formidable general to face in combat. The two armies first clashed not far from Rochester. Fairfax, who had never been known to lose a battle, slowly but surely drove the enemy back towards Maidstone. Then, at seven o'clock in the evening on 1 June, about a mile outside the town, a fierce battle was joined. On home ground, the Kentish forces hid behind thickets, hedgerows and barns shooting wildly at Black Tom's troops. Returning fire the more disciplined troops of the New Model Army gradually forced the Royalists into the town itself.

Dark storm clouds now began to shroud the scene as the clash of arms rung from every street corner. As night fell, the desperate fighting continued. Infantry men battled it out in face-to-face encounters in the narrow alleyways. To add to the confusion torrential rain began cascading down, making it almost impossible to tell friend from foe. And still the men struggled on. At last, at one o'clock in the morning, victory was declared for Fairfax and his troops. The roar of cannons subsided, the wild neighing of frightened horses and the screams of wounded and dying men faded away. An eerie silence followed on that June night in 1648. The streets of Maidstone were littered with dead bodies — casualties of one of the bloodiest encounters of the Second Civil War.

But the task of rounding up weary, bedraggled and wounded men, hiding in ditches, backyards and fields, went on all night. Morning light revealed more than three hundred soldiers dead, their bodies lying in field and street. In addition, some 1400 men were captured and taken prisoner. The Battle of Maidstone was over, but the cost in human life and suffering was not.

'Bloody Newes from Kent' ran the title of a communication sent from the battlefield to London. But General Fairfax, a just and upright Christian man, did not exact vengeance on his prisoners. Instead he sent them all to their homes, only detaining twelve men whom he judged to be ringleaders and chief perpetrators in the uprising. These were destined for the gallows — a terrible spectacle designed to prevent any further rebellion.

Major John Gifford was among the men handpicked for execution. Together with eleven others he was cast into the Maidstone town jail. Here he had time to meditate on his imminent death, and the hereafter that awaited him. Closely guarded night and day, there could be no escape. A heavy drinker, Gifford might well have decided that the best way to cope with his forthcoming appointment with the gallows was to become inebriated. Strange to say, he acted out of character and remained sober. A few nights later the captured men were informed that they would die at first light. Gifford had a sister living in the town, and hearing that her brother was to perish publicly in the morning she contrived to enter the prison to say her last farewells.

A surprise awaited the young woman at the gate of the prison. The guards, instead of being on duty and alert, were slumped in heavy slumber at their posts. With little difficulty Ann Gifford passed through the gates. The noise of drunken laughter greeted her as she approached the cell where the men were being held. All except John were intoxicated. At that moment a daring plan entered the young woman's head. In an excited whisper she told John of the sleeping guards at the gate and urged him to make a speedy escape while the opportunity remained. Stunned at the news, John acted quickly, following her out of the cell. Silently they slipped past the guards, still heavily asleep, out through the darkened streets and into the countryside.

But where could he hide? A shallow rain-soaked ditch seemed the only answer, for undoubtedly Ann Gifford's house would be the first place to be searched for the missing prisoner. As morning light broke, the condemned men were led one by one from the cells to the gallows, erected where all might see the fearsome end of such rebellion. Why were there only eleven prisoners? Where was the twelfth and who was missing? It took only a few moments to discover that Major John Gifford was nowhere to be found.

Before long a search had begun. Every street, every barn was ransacked to find the missing man. Out into the fields and woods they rode, examining trenches, hedgerows, woods, but all in vain. At times they may have come very close to the damp ditch where Gifford lay concealed, but they did not find him. With nothing to eat and only rain water to alleviate his thirst, it was a test of endurance for the escapee. At last after three days the search was called off, for surely John Gifford must be far away by now. How he survived such circumstances we may never know.

With the help of a few friends Gifford left his ditch and, disguised as a working man, he made his way to London. Here he hid for some time, but London was no safe place to stay for the city was seething with unrest, and it was hard to know whom one could trust. The runaway major must find some bolt-hole where friends could protect him until the situation was

John Gifford

Old Bedford town

calm once more. And what better place than Bedford, a quiet community largely supporting the Parliamentarian cause? No one would think of searching for him there; and even better, he had friends in the town who had defended the Royalists.

An educated man, John Gifford had acquired some knowledge of medicine and before long he discovered that Bedford's elderly town physician, Francis Bannister, wished to give up his position. Here then was Gifford's opportunity, and he soon set himself up as physician in place of Bannister and began dispensing medicines and advice to the unsuspecting people of Bedford.

Despite escaping certain death on the gallows, surviving for three days in a damp ditch and discovering friends who would protect him, Gifford's nature was no more subdued by a sense of God's mercy than that of a tiger in captivity. Before long his vicious and profligate habits gained the upper hand once more. Cursing, drunkenness and gambling for ever higher stakes became a way of life for the ex-Royalist major. What little he earned as he dispensed his medicines he lost at the gambling tables. How his young wife reacted to the realization that she had married a ne'er-do-well and a rogue, we cannot say.

Added to this there was a simmering hatred growing in John Gifford's heart for all men of Puritan persuasion. Had not a Puritan, General Fairfax, quelled the uprising in Maidstone, killing many of his associates? A desire for revenge burned in his mind. He had an overwhelming urge to kill in return. But who should be the target of his vengeance? Gradually his mind focussed on one man — a man by the name of Anthony Harrington; and for no other reason except that he was an earnest and upright Christian — one of the leading Puritans of Bedford. More than this, he learnt that Harrington was one of a small group of men and women who met together from time to time to share their Christian experience and to encourage each other in their common faith. Surely here was a man ripe for assassination, thought Gifford, as dark murderous plans filled his mind.

Each time John Gifford lost at the gambling table, he made some feeble resolution to break the habit; but no sooner had he some more money in his pocket than he was back again. It seemed that the chains of this evil practice held him captive. But one night something happened which snapped those chains for ever. As usual he was back, dicing desperately to recoup his losses. One final throw would surely change his luck. It did not. In fact he lost £15.00 — a colossal sum of money in days when a labouring man's wage might be as little as £5.00 a year.

In a frenzy of rage John Gifford cursed his God — a thing that not even he had dared to do before. Returning to his home, his mind was filled with dark and angry thoughts against God, the one who had preserved his life in so amazing a way and had borne with him in spite of all. Whether his wife was a secret believer, we do not know, but at this critical juncture

John Gifford

Gifford picked up a book written by a Puritan preacher and scholar, Robert Bolton. On the fly leaf he read the title, *The last and learned worke of the Foure last Things: Death, Judgement, Hell and Heaven*. A less likely book to attract the attention of the prodigal Puritan-hater, it is hard to imagine. But a power greater than he knew was at work. 'Death, judgement and hell', yes, he had certainly come face to face with death, and perhaps God had condemned him to both judgement and hell for his wicked ways.

Turning over the pages, he discovered sentence after sentence that pierced through his soul like an arrow to its mark: 'Consider that to die is but to be done once, and if we err in that one action we are undone everlastingly. What manner of man ought you to be in the mean time ... to give up your account with comfort at that dreadful hour?' But not only did the writer convict Gifford of his wayward life and the weight of his sins, he also pointed out the path of deliverance. Christ has invited all sinners, even those 'readier far to sink into the bottom of hell' because of their 'impure, abominable and beastly' sins, to come to him. Through the blood of his cross he was ready to forgive those who were conscious of their 'unfitness, unworthiness, vileness and wretchedness'.

Night after night this poor broken man pondered over the small print of Bolton's book, seizing desperately at the hope it proclaimed for the penitent. For about a month he read, meditated and prayed. Perhaps there might yet be mercy, even for so flagrant a sinner as John Gifford. And at last the light and joy of forgiveness broke into his darkness — such joy as he could scarcely contain.

With the establishment of the Commonwealth and the end of the Second Civil War, it appears that John Gifford was no longer a wanted man. And now his great desire was to serve the God who had not only spared him from the hangman, but dealt with him in grace. His strong desire was to share with fellow believers God's amazing mercy to him. But to whom could he go? Gifford knew of no others save that despised group of men and women of whom Anthony Harrington was one. But surely they would not accept him or believe him. His former hatred of one of their number was well known. Yet he must try. Not surprisingly, John Gifford was turned away abruptly. This must certainly be some plot, they thought, some attempt to spy on their secret gatherings and cause trouble for them. The days were still dangerous and unsettled, with turmoil and unrest in many parts following the execution of Charles I in January 1649.

In spite of their protests these people found to their dismay this unwanted intruder gathering with them as they met together week by week. Wary and suspicious of his motives, they made it quite clear that he was not welcome. Like Saul of Tarsus when he tried to join the Christians of Damascus and Jerusalem, Gifford too was finding it hard to win the confidence of the believers of Bedford. But gradually, one by one, as they heard him speak of his experience and caught the radiant joy of his profession of faith, they began to accept Gifford among them.

With a hungry heart and diligent desire, the new convert started to study the Bible, and soon gained a masterly grasp of its truths. No longer a young man, he knew his time could be short. If only he could preach that same gospel that he had once despised and bring others to know forgiveness of sins as well. Approaching the subject with one and another of the Bedford believers, now his closest friends, Gifford was gladdened by the encouragement they gave him. And on his very first attempt to preach, a young woman was converted. What better sign could he want that God was calling him to give the remainder of his life to preaching those truths he had once laboured to destroy?

A natural leader, Gifford soon came to see that this small group of men and women, scarcely more than twelve in number, needed to be formed into a viable church fellowship which could meet regularly for worship. Together they talked and prayed over it and under Gifford's guidance fundamental principles of church life were laid down. Only one condition would be required for membership of this emerging fellowship: genuine faith in Christ, together with holiness of life as evidence of that faith. Even though baptism by immersion of those who had professed faith was to be their practice, none would be excluded from their communion services because they had not been baptized or had been baptized as infants.

If they were to form a new church, they would need a pastor to minister to them on a regular basis. And who better than John Gifford himself? Like many late converts, the wonder of the grace of God towards him had never ceased to amaze him, and it is recorded of this former Royalist major that 'all his life thereafter he never lost the light of God's countenance'. During the days of Oliver Cromwell's Commonwealth any viable congregation, whether Anglican or Independent, could be granted the use of a parish church building. Several members of the Bedford Meeting, as they were soon to be called, had held important positions in the town and so it was that in 1653 the Bedford Corporation bestowed the living of St John's, one of five parish churches in the town, on John Gifford and his congregation. Soon Gifford, his wife and three young daughters moved into St John's Rectory attached to the church. And on Sundays this new congregation found themselves sitting on the high-backed hard pews, listening in rapt attention to their pastor who had already earned the name of 'holy Mr Gifford'.

Questions of deep Christian experience were paramount to these members of the new Bedford Meeting: subjects such as the wretchedness of their own hearts by nature and the necessity of the new birth; of how God had visited their souls with his love; of his help in their trials and difficulties; of the comforts he had showered on them; of the subtle temptations

St John's Rectory, Bedford

of Satan; and of how they had been refreshed and strengthened by the promises of Scripture.

On one occasion, as two or three of the women members of the church were sitting outside their cottages in the sunshine sharing such things with each other, they noticed a young man lingering not far away, just within earshot. A tall well-built fellow with auburn hair, he appeared to be highly interested in their conversation. Perhaps he was spying on them. But day after day it was the same. Whenever they took a break from their work, snatching a few minutes to talk together, this same young man always seemed to be around. Soon they learnt that he was a brazier or tinker who had come into Bedford from nearby Elstow in the course of his work which was to mend pots and pans. His name was John Bunyan.

Before long the women of the Bedford Meeting realized that the young brazier was no idle passer-by, but a man deeply troubled about his own spiritual state. Gradually, as he grew more confident, he began to ask them questions — profound perplexing questions for which they had no immediate answers: How can I know whether I have faith or not? How can I tell whether God has chosen me for salvation? Perhaps he has already saved all the people he wants in these parts. What if he never calls me? Have I committed the unforgivable sin? Sensibly the women decided that the only person who would be able to answer the tinker's questions was their pastor, John Gifford.

Hour after hour Gifford sat and reasoned with the tormented young man, patiently listening to his multitude of anxieties. He allowed him to sit quietly in the room while he dealt with the spiritual problems of others so that Bunyan could see that his own were not unique. Gifford learnt that the younger man carried a heavy burden of guilt for he had been one of life's 'wasters', in fact a ringleader in his village community for all that was godless and profane. And was not John Gifford the right man to help such a person for he too had a grievous past record of corrupt and evil behaviour? Far from despairing about the young tinker, though he had probably never met anyone with so many fears and complex obsessions, he was convinced that here was one whom God was singling out for exceptional usefulness in his kingdom. For two years John Gifford patiently counselled John Bunyan, until at last the younger man attained a measure of assurance as he eventually saw that all the goodness which God requires in order to accept a sinner has been provided in the person of his Son, Jesus Christ. One dark night in 1653 the older John baptized the younger John, as tradition tells us, in the waters of an inlet of the River Great Ouse near Duck Mill Lane.

John Bunyan became a member of the Bedford Meeting and his name is found at number twenty-six on the church roll. Patiently and kindly the other members encouraged and supported their new member and the example of his first pastor, 'holy Mr Gifford', became John Bunyan's role model. His influence on him was profound. Undoubtedly when he wrote *The Pilgrim's Progress* many years later, Bunyan had Gifford in mind as he described the type of guide his pilgrim must follow. Gazing at the portrait of the 'very grave person' at the House of the Interpreter, 'Christian' noted that:

Site of Bunyan's baptism by Gifford

his eyes [were] lifted up to heaven, the best of Books in
his hand, the law of truth was written upon his lips, the
world behind his back; he stood as if he pleaded with
men, and a crown of gold did hang over his head.

'I have showed thee this picture first,' said the Interpreter,
'because the man whose picture this is, is the only man whom
the Lord of the place where you are going has authorised to be
your guide in all difficult places that you may meet with in the
way.'

Sadly John Gifford could not be John Bunyan's guide for
long. Only two more years of life remained to him after Bunyan
had joined the Bedford Meeting. Gifford was not an old man,
probably little more than fifty, when in 1655 he realized that
he had a terminal illness. Troubling thoughts raced through
his mind: the young church at Bedford needed him so much;
stormy days might lie ahead for these Christian men and
women. What would happen to the country if Oliver Cromwell
died? Would Charles I's playboy son be invited to take the
crown? Would persecution follow? Gifford did not know. Of

one thing only he seemed sure: that he had run his race and must now hand over the leadership of the infant church to others. The fact that John Bunyan was among the membership and was already beginning to preach with marked effect must have been a great consolation.

John Bunyan

Anxious to leave behind some guidelines for his small congregation, with great difficulty Gifford wrote a parting letter which they could read out at their church gatherings when he had left them for ever. Like the apostle Paul, whom Gifford had resembled in certain respects, his letter had an almost apostolic ring:

> To the church over which God has made me an overseer when I was in the world ... I beseech you, brethren beloved, let these words (written in my love to you and care over you when our heavenly Father was removing me to the kingdom of his dear Son) be read at your gatherings together... Be constant in your church assemblies ... let all the work which concerns the church be done faithfully among you... Let no respect of persons be in your comings together; when you are met together there is neither rich nor poor, bond nor free... Spend much time before the Lord about choosing a pastor...

Detailed instructions followed about conditions for church membership, prayer, and most of all the urgent need to preserve love and unity among themselves — a wise, pastoral letter from

The rectory garden where 'holy Mr Gifford' talked with John Bunyan

a dying man. Moments after reading his parting charge to the men and women whom he had led and guided, now gathered at his bedside, John Gifford was taken from them. And many years later the mantle of leadership for the Bedford Meeting *did* fall on the shoulders of John Bunyan — for whom the memory of 'holy Mr Gifford' was one he could never erase from his memory.

Only seven years earlier Gifford's life had been saved from the hangman's noose and soon afterwards his soul snatched from the clutches of Satan. Not only had God purposes of mercy for Gifford himself and for the Bedford church, but he had far wider blessings in store for the whole church of Jesus Christ through the influence and writings of a greater than Gifford, the converted tinker of Elstow, John Bunyan.

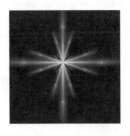

Fanny Guinness

in the shadow of
a great man

*Orphaned at a young age, Fanny Fitzgerald would
marry Henry Grattan Guinness, outstanding
preacher, and Director of the East London Institute.
Her sacrificial contribution to the institute, with its
remarkable role in the huge expansion of missionary
endeavour during the late nineteenth century, well
deserves to be remembered and celebrated.*

Fanny Guinness
(1832-1898)

in the shadow
of a great man

Major Edward Fitzgerald could think of no solution to his problems. Broken and desolate, he wrote a final plea begging someone to care for his four orphaned daughters after his death. Then he leapt into the sea from the deck of a cross-Channel steamer.

From an aristocratic Irish family, Major Fitzgerald, an erect, handsome military man, had suddenly found himself in great distress. The death of his wife Mabel from the scourge of tuberculosis had left him with the sole responsibility for their five children: his eldest, Gerald, still only ten years of age, together with four small girls. Fitzgerald manfully undertook the care and provision for his family as best he could but at times his situation had seemed unendurable. Turning to journalism as a source of income, he had become an acceptable writer and an editor of a Dublin newspaper. His children could still remember him as he sat at the family table late into the night under the flickering light of a candle: writing, writing, always writing...

Then in 1840 a further serious blow had struck the family — an outbreak of smallpox. Gerald, now twelve, and his eight-year-old sister Fanny both fell victim to the virulent infection. Battling against a soaring fever, Fanny was scarcely aware of the moment when her brother was carried away from the bed they were sharing. Only when she had recovered sufficiently was she told that Gerald had died.

This last tragedy had been too much for Edward Fitzgerald, and had led to that final reckless action. But how could he realistically have supposed that anyone would undertake the care of his four girls? Certainly it seemed an unpromising start to life for Fanny, his second daughter, and for her sisters. But God had special purposes for Fanny and in an unexpected way a London banker, sitting reading his newspaper in his office one morning, was moved with pity as he noted the sad story. Thoughtfully Arthur West went home and showed his wife Mary the article. Could *they* do anything to help? Childless themselves, their pleasant home in Stamford Hill, London, often seemed empty. Both Mary and her husband, a Quaker couple, had longed for children.

Not a day had passed before Mary was out contacting a number of her Quaker friends and had soon found suitable homes for three of the Fitzgerald girls. And eight-year-old Fanny, her intelligent grey eyes and expressive features compensating for her rather plain appearance, was taken in by Arthur and Mary West themselves, to be brought up as their own daughter. Nor did the sisters lose contact with each other, despite being in separate families.

Fanny Fitzgerald found herself surrounded by circumstances which encouraged her bright inquisitive mind, her literary abilities and her strong independent spirit. Spiritually too, influences on the child had lifelong implications. These were the days of the early Brethren movement: a reaction to the decadence of the Established Church. Simultaneously groups of Christians had gathered together in various locations, anxious to restore the simplicity of New Testament worship. One of the main centres was Fanny's own native Dublin. By the 1840s the movement had spread and was gathering adherents in many places, particularly Plymouth. And with their appreciation of unadorned worship, Arthur and Mary West found themselves attracted to the Brethren and took Fanny with them to their nearest assembly.

Fanny repaid in full the kindness shown to her by her guardians. When Arthur later suffered a debilitating stroke, she helped Mary to care for him, taking a job as a teacher to augment the family's income. Tragically, unable to cope with his own limitations any longer, Arthur, like Fanny's father, also took his own life. And when Mary herself became ill, Fanny devoted her time and strength towards making Mary's declining years as easy as possible. Now a sincere and earnest Christian, Fanny continued to attend the Brethren assembly, this time in Bath where they were living. Despite her undeniable debt to the biblical teaching and example of the members of the assembly, there was something about their emphasis that seemed to stifle the natural flair and fervour of Fanny's Irish personality. Demure, diligent and dutiful in her behaviour, it was as if she needed something or someone to kindle the fire latent within her make-up. But nothing could have prepared the young woman, now twenty-nine years of age, for the changes soon to transform her life.

These were the days when the great spiritual revival which began in the late 1850s was sweeping across the land. And one of the most outstanding preachers raised up by God was a young man by the name of Henry Grattan Guinness. A nephew of Arthur Guinness of the famous brewing Guinness family of

Dublin, Henry Grattan was travelling the country, preaching to vast congregations. In February 1858 the twenty-three-year-old preacher arrived in Dublin. A Guinness family member who preached the gospel rather than sell beer was certainly a new phenomenon. Henry's outstanding preaching gifts immediately drew the people, leading his hearers to couple his name with that of C. H. Spurgeon, his senior by only a few months. In Belfast later that same year crowds of up to 20,000 were crushed into the Botanic Gardens to hear Henry Guinness. And so it continued, until by the summer of 1860 Henry was in urgent need of a holiday.

Even on holiday in Ilfracombe, Devon, he seized opportunities to preach, and one young woman, also on holiday there, heard him. Laura Fitzgerald could not stop talking about the young preacher, describing his virtues in glowing terms to her sisters who were on holiday with her. And little wonder. His handsome appearance, black wavy hair swept back from his face, his graceful gestures and attractive Irish lilt had quite turned the young woman's head. But her sister Fanny Fitzgerald was unimpressed.

As the Fitzgerald sisters sat together on the cliff top one day, a small boat came into view with a single rower. 'That's him!' gasped Laura in astonishment as she recognized the dark-haired oarsman before he disappeared from view. 'That youth?' remarked Fanny with a note of disdain in her voice.

Not many days later all was to change. Henry Grattan Guinness was introduced to the Fitzgerald sisters by a mutual friend at the Brethren Hall. But it was not Laura that attracted his attention. It was Fanny. Henry looked beyond the careworn exterior, beyond the plain if bashful appearance, and saw something to which his soul responded with fervour and love. 'I felt I had found for the first time in my life a woman with a mind and soul that answered my own,' he would later say. Only two months after this, in October 1860, Fanny Fitzgerald married Henry Guinness.

And a strange wedding it was — conducted without adornment: no flowers, no music, no one to officiate, just two chairs placed centrally for the bride and groom, with friends and family gathered around. After vows were exchanged with prayer and hymns sung unaccompanied, Henry and Fanny were declared man and wife. So began years of extraordinary usefulness in the service of the kingdom of God for Fanny

Fanny Guinness

Guinness — despite a life lived in the shadow of a great and unpredictable man.

A carefree honeymoon over, Henry and Fanny were soon plunged into a crucible of troubles, the first and most serious resulting from Henry's alarming loss of popularity as a preacher. His marriage to Fanny inevitably brought him into contact with her Brethren friends, and a stigma of sectarianism attached to that infant church grouping made many congregations suspicious of him. But more critical was the effect which his new friends were to have on Henry's own preaching. Sensitive and concerned to please God in all things, the young preacher was deeply disturbed when members of the assembly suggested that his oratorical pulpit gifts were an expression of pride and any 'liberty' in preaching a sign of self-indulgence. The result was an alarming loss of power in the pulpit as Henry tried to crush his freedom of expression and soon developed an entirely uncharacteristic hesitancy. Rarely would Henry Grattan Guinness ever regain his previously eloquent delivery.

At the same time the early Brethren movement was fascinated with unfulfilled prophecy, and with his own interest kindled, this became the dominant theme of all Henry's future writings and ministry. Within months of his marriage he was to publish his first pamphlet on the subject. A second tour of America, undertaken in 1861, this time accompanied by Fanny, also turned into a disaster as the young preacher ventured into the political arena and criticized the emergent attitudes of the Northern states to the Southern over the slavery issue.

Virtually frozen out of the States by public opinion, Henry and Fanny went to Canada where their first child, also named Henry Grattan, was born. Canada offered little consolation to the dispirited preacher and before long Henry's spirits were so low that a return to England became imperative. With no income, few preaching engagements, and a second child on the way, it took all Fanny's resourcefulness to bolster Henry's confidence. But God was watching over this young family and a tour of Palestine, financed by a friend, followed by an enthusiastic welcome in Liverpool, did much to restore Henry's naturally buoyant spirit. The safe birth of a daughter, named Geraldine — perhaps in memory of Fanny's brother — was an added bonus.

Two or three uncertain years were to follow as the family moved from place to place wherever Henry could find evangelistic opportunities. At last in 1865 he decided to move to Dublin, for now another ambition was dominating his thinking. With the publication in 1859 of Charles Darwin's work *On the Origin of Species,* a tide of unbelief and scepticism was sweeping through the country, undermining the faith of many. Henry planned to start a small training scheme to give young Christian men sufficient theological instruction to enable them to counter the current biblical criticism.

So with the birth of her third child now imminent, Fanny patiently moved yet again and the family found rented accommodation in one of the poorer parts of Dublin. A few weeks later Lucy was born, a frail child, but one whose sensitivity, gifts and potential would bring much delight to Fanny and Henry. Before long Henry had gathered a group of young men around him, including the quixotic, bespectacled Tom Barnardo, who would prove a lifelong friend.

Concern for the unevangelized parts of the earth was also running high among Christians, an outcome of the powerful converting work that had brought many to faith during the revival. When Henry Guinness introduced Hudson Taylor, who had been doing pioneer work in China, to his Dublin group the result was unanticipated. Taylor was eagerly seeking recruits to work as missionaries in the vast unreached areas of inland China and the effect of his words was such that not only did Tom Barnardo volunteer but Henry and Fanny too wished to leave all and accompany Hudson Taylor to that distant land.

After careful thought Taylor decided to decline their offer, but did suggest that possibly they could train young men for the mission field instead. Although only a seed thought, in due time it would bear astonishing fruit and lead to a life work for Henry and Fanny which would have a profound effect in spreading the Christian gospel in many of the most hostile and inaccessible places on earth.

Restless as ever, Henry Guinness seemed unable to stay in any one place for long. New horizons, new evangelistic opportunities continued to beckon him irresistibly onwards. During the next six years Fanny heroically accompanied her husband from place to place, together with her ever-increasing family, despite her longing for a settled home. Two years were spent in Paris where they both learnt the language and Henry established a small church. Here two more children were born:

Gershom, known later by his second name, Whitfield; and a third daughter, Phoebe. Fanny and Henry would have stayed longer had not the Franco-Prussian war broken out in 1870. But with danger threatening on every hand, they knew they must bring their young family back to the safety of England. From their home in Bath, they listened with increasing horror to news of the fearsome Siege of Paris and the devastation wreaked on that beautiful city.

With the birth of their last child, Agnes, in Bath the family now numbered six children, all under the age of ten. The earlier loss of a five-month-old baby whom they had named Henrietta was a grief that Fanny found hard to forget. Although life was often spartan and uncertain for the family, it was a happy home and Fanny, despite her own chequered childhood, was a mother of deep kindness and understanding. Before their eyes the Guinness children saw an example of selfless love to the Saviour: a bedrock for their own lives.

Calm, practical and competent, Fanny was also ideally suited as a foil to the erratic genius of Henry Grattan. The cataclysmic events in Europe, with the rise and unification of Germany under

Fanny and her children

Bismarck and the loss of the Vatican's political clout as it became absorbed into the state of Italy, fuelled Henry's fascination with unfulfilled prophecy. Surely these things must indicate an approaching end of the world! Day by day Henry could be found studying and writing as his influential masterpiece, *The Approaching End of the Age,* gradually took shape.

But God had hidden purposes yet for this gifted wandering evangelist and his remarkable wife — and Armagh in Ireland was the place in which he chose to stop Henry Grattan Guinness in his tracks and give him a new direction for his entire life. As Henry, now thirty-five years of age, walked around the centre of Armagh pondering his future, the suggestion which Hudson Taylor had set before the would-be missionaries in 1865, that of training others for the mission field, suddenly flashed before Henry's eyes with all the clarity of a vision. Now he knew. 'The cloud moves,' he wrote in his journal that night, 'may I have grace to follow.'

Where that cloud was moving, Fanny Guinness scarcely knew, but she too would need much grace to follow. She soon discovered that this next step would take her, together with her six young children, away from the relative comfort of Bath into one of the most sordid and unattractive parts of the country: the East End of London.

What better place to train young potential missionaries, destined to labour in some of the darkest places on earth, than the East End, thought Henry Guinness. Raw, rowdy, deprived and wretched, the population that crammed into the area around Mile End Road was needy enough, and his spirit rose to the challenge. It would certainly be an ideal centre for preaching in the open air.

Fanny struggled to face such a situation bravely as she accompanied Henry in search of suitable accommodation for their prospective college. 'I feel just like a would-be swimmer, longing to strike out and feel the water up-bearing him, yet fearing to trust himself to do it,' she confided to the pages of her diary. Fanny knew well that the burden of management and provision would fall heavily upon her shoulders, for her visionary husband was not geared for such practical considerations. 'But,' she added valiantly, 'I shall swim yet.'

The new college was to be called the East London Institute, and after much searching a large if shabby house was found in Stepney Green that would suit the purpose. Towards the end of 1872 the family moved to London with Fanny making the rooms ready to accept their first students. Nine small bedrooms with few furnishings other than a narrow bed, a table and a lamp would be quite adequate for future missionaries, thought Henry and Fanny. Three studies and a dining room sufficient to seat twenty made the accommodation seem yet more suitable, and in January 1873 the first student arrived. Joshua Chowriappah, a young Indian man with scarcely enough English to make himself understood, seemed a strange first choice, but the children loved him.

Soon volunteers from many different nations applied for admission and during the first year thirty-two young men received basic biblical and missionary training under the guidance of Henry Guinness. Their life work had begun. None other than the volatile Tom Barnardo, now engaged in the rescue of destitute children, was to become co-director of the work. With 'his beaming face, cheery voice, broad brow, big brain, glowing heart and indomitable courage', Barnardo was a family favourite.

Following Hudson Taylor's precept of never making any direct appeals for money, the burden of the finance for the fledgling college fell heavily on Fanny. To feed thirty young men adequately was no small challenge, and yet Fanny rose to it. She would later write, 'We began the Institute with nothing in hand — no premises, no furniture, no linen, china, cutlery, no educational apparatus ... without funds in hand, but with the conviction that if it were of God and for his glory, he would send the means of supply.' And he did. During the first year gifts were received from more than two hundred donors, and before many months had passed four young men left the college for distant mission fields.

Criticisms from the wider family reached Fanny. Had she not thought of the effects of rearing a young family in such an environment? What about schooling for the children? Infectious diseases were rife in the crowded tenements; had she considered the consequences of her actions? Yes, Fanny agreed, it was not ideal, but there was a robust strain in her make-up which enabled her to make light of such censures, confident that the God who had directed them would make provision for their needs.

Scarcely a year had passed before the house in Stepney Green was too small to meet the ever-increasing demand as young men applied for training. Because the Guinnesses charged the students no fees, many with a passion for the spread of the Christian gospel could take advantage of the courses who would never be able to contemplate normal college charges. At the very time when their need for more accommodation became most acute, premises known as Harley House, situated just two miles away off the Bow Road, became available.

Noisy, it certainly was, with the Bryant and May match factory nearby, the Tower of London not far distant and the ceaseless flow of cab wheels grating on the uneven road surface. But Harley House was ideally suited to their needs. Most of the students still slept at Stepney Green, with lectures and meals at Harley. Family accommodation was on the first floor, and the back garden was spacious and attractive. The only problem was that Henry and Fanny had insufficient funds to furnish their new home. But Fanny, upon whom the main burden fell, had long since discovered that the God who hears prayer could supply their every need.

Harley House

Before long curtains were hanging at the windows, and chairs, desks, tables and a host of other necessities were provided, most often by the generosity of friends who were far from well-off themselves. Sometimes, however, her faith wavered and she would write in despair to Henry who was travelling the country preaching and recruiting new students, telling of her predicament. Sacrifice was therefore often the order of the day for the Guinness family and the students. Fanny detested debt and if there was not enough money to buy adequate food, meat and any other perceived luxury would disappear off the menu. But strangely, unaccountably, needs were met and still more students applied for places at Harley College. First one, then two and then yet another adjoining property was purchased and added to the college, with a new wing built on for extra sleeping accommodation. Within the first fourteen years of the opening of the college, over five hundred young men had been trained and were now battling through jungles into the heart of Africa, settling in primitive huts, often dying of strange tropical diseases, all to reach men and women with the liberating gospel of Jesus Christ.[1]

In 1875, only two years after the opening of Harley College, Henry and Fanny Guinness received a remarkable gift. An elderly couple owned an extensive, if rambling, estate called Cliff House, in Hope Valley, five miles from Bakewell, in the unspoilt Peak District of Derbyshire. No longer able to maintain the property, and with no family to whom to leave it, the couple felt certain that the estate could be used in Christian service — perhaps as a training college for missionary candidates. Following the death of the owner, his widow offered Cliff House to the Guinnesses for the use of the students. Perched on rocky cliffs high above the River Derwent, the house commanded panoramic views of the river and the hills beyond. To a family from the East End of London, Cliff College, as it was quickly renamed, brought welcome and necessary relief from the sights and sounds of the slums of London. For Fanny, often overworked and burdened, it was both therapeutic and a tangible evidence of the care and love of God. Far from the nightly throb of traffic, Fanny could write, 'Night brings real silence. Your whole being seems to expand with a sense of relief.'

What better training, thought Henry, for would-be missionaries than to learn all the practical skills required in the renovation and upkeep of such a place. Here they could practise survival techniques as they bred pigs, milked cows and planted crops. For Henry too it was a place where he could relax from the demands of his preaching and teaching, and concentrate on his prophetic writings. But such pleasures did not come without their anxieties, and these Fanny bore nobly and silently as she wondered time and time again how she could possibly finance the extra costs, in addition to all the other expenditures of their burgeoning work. Her diary tells its own tale: 'No money came in today; we have not a week's expenses in hand, with a hundred people dependent, in a sense, on us.' And yet the needs were met.

Opportunities for expansion of the college and further evangelistic endeavours brought new impetus and challenge to Henry Guinness, and while he dreamed the dreams of new openings for the gospel, the details of organization fell to his practical wife. Much in demand as a preacher since the publication of his book *The Approaching End of the Age* in 1878, Henry was still absorbed in the subject of unfulfilled prophecy. Gazing through a large and expensive telescope — his most treasured possession — he scanned the night skies with increasing fascination.[2] Nor were his ideas mere idle speculations. Based on careful biblical study, particularly of the books of Daniel and of Revelation, he would propose an interpretation of the mysterious and coded dating of God's future purposes revealed to both Daniel and the apostle John.[3] To Fanny fell the task of editing and rewriting Henry's erudite prophecies into language which the ordinary reader could follow. Amid popular acclaim, the book was reprinted five times within eighteen months, so great was the demand. And in turn the Christian public became yet more aware of the sterling work of Henry and Fanny as they trained an ever-increasing number of young men.

Cliff College continued to provide welcome respite for hard-pressed Fanny and Henry Guinness, as well as valuable training for the students. Fanny's two youngest girls, Agnes and Phoebe, aged five and six, found great delight in the freedom and beauty of Cliff and, as children do, followed the students around, even into the milking sheds and pigsties, always watching and trying to help.

But a tragedy of enormous proportions was soon to strike the family. Early in 1879 Henry was away preaching and had taken Gershom with him. On the morning of their departure Agnes, now six, had complained of a headache and sore throat. Suspecting nothing serious, Fanny left the child in the care of seventeen-year-old Geraldine and went out. But when her condition deteriorated over the next couple of days, Fanny became anxious and called a doctor. He diagnosed tonsillitis, but Fanny feared it might be something worse. What if her cheerful little girl had contracted diphtheria?

As Agnes's breathing became more laboured, Fanny's worst fears were realized. She sent an urgent message to Henry summoning him home. The doctor performed an emergency tracheotomy to relieve the child's breathing, yet still the infection spread. Then to Fanny's distress, both Phoebe and Geraldine succumbed to the dreaded infection. But when Fanny felt her own throat becoming sore as her temperature rose, Harley House was evacuated, the students sent to their homes, and Lucy to relatives. As for Fanny, the doctor forbade her to go near her sick children. Henry returned as soon as possible but although Geraldine was holding her own against the disease, it was now clear that both of the two younger girls were dying. Disobeying the doctor, Fanny sat beside Phoebe trying to cool her feverish body, while Henry stood helplessly at the door, forbidden to go near. Too stunned to cry, Fanny remained by Phoebe for some time after the child had died. Then giving her a last kiss, she rose heavily and went to Agnes's bedside and sat with her until the end. Agnes died just ten hours after her older sister. Fanny and Henry had lost their two youngest children in one short day. Weakened with illness and sorrow, Fanny and Geraldine wept together through the long night that followed. And we can imagine Henry pacing restlessly back and forth in an agony of grief, not being allowed to come near his wife and elder daughter for fear of infection.

The pain of her bereavement remained a scar on Fanny Guinness's mind. Many parents lost their children in the disease-ridden slums of London in those days, but this made it no easier to bear. 'Children are winged joys, ready at a moment's notice to take their flight,' she wrote, and even through her tears

Lucy with Agnes and Phoebe

she acknowledged that the goodness of God and his purposes — though mysterious at times — are right. Geraldine recovered and providentially Harry, Lucy and Gershom had been kept clear of the infection. Perhaps God yet had purposes for these four.

He had indeed. For the Guinness children such an upbringing as theirs had early taught them the meaning of sacrifice for Christ's sake. They followed the progress of 'their' missionaries, praying for them in dangerous situations and grieving over the setbacks. Remarkably gifted and highly intelligent, each of them would make a significant contribution to the Christian church. Harry, the eldest, after training as a doctor, did pioneer work in the Congo before taking over the running of Harley House from his parents; Geraldine, as a missionary in China, married Hudson Taylor's son, Howard, then devoted herself to literary work, writing her well-known biography of Hudson Taylor's life and the development of the China Inland Mission; Gershom Whitfield, also a missionary doctor with the China Inland Mission, narrowly escaped death during the Boxer Uprising in

1900, and founded the first hospital in Henan province. Lucy would marry a pioneer missionary, Karl Kumm, founder of the Sudan United Mission, and devote her short intense life to literary work on behalf of missions.

Fanny meanwhile flung herself into the work at Harley House with added diligence. The work was expanding in many different directions. Other evangelistic agencies opened up as the influence of Harley Institute grew yet more extensive. Mission halls, evening classes for the deprived factory girls of Bryant and May, schools for the destitute of the East End — all could be traced back to the work of the Harley students. It has been estimated that 12,000 people were reached each week with the message of the gospel of Christ in one or other of these evangelistic endeavours.

The Livingstone Inland Mission was founded in 1878 as Harley House students fought their way through the dense jungles of Africa's heartland; even a steamer named *The Livingstone,* to carry young missionary volunteers along the treacherous waters of the Congo River, was added to their multitude of enterprises. And always Henry was the figurehead of these endeavours, with his wife Fanny at her desk, writing reports, toiling over the finances. She could say from experience, 'Devotedness and consecration to Jesus ... means stern labour, and toil, it means constant self-denial, and self-sacrifice, it means unwearied well-doing even unto death.'

Henry Grattan Guinness

The years passed and by the time Fanny Guinness was sixty-one she was worn out. A life poured out in selfless sacrifice for others had taken its toll and in early 1892 she suffered a severe stroke. Deprived of speech and mobility, her life hung in the balance. Henry was abroad at the time, Lucy on a speaking tour in America, Geraldine a missionary in China, and Harry in the Congo. All came home to be with their mother. In the event Fanny gradually regained partial speech, but would remain paralysed down one side. No more would she be able to carry the burden of work and administration. Cliff College, with its unspoilt beauty and silence, became a haven for the sick woman. Henry grieved deeply over the changes and sufferings of the one he had loved and relied upon. Still able to continue with his work, he spent much time abroad, frequently accompanied by Lucy, promoting the work of Christian missions.

Fanny kept in touch with her children, writing letters and praying for them. That each should be serving that same cause to which she had devoted her life was her greatest consolation. Perhaps the most moving expression of it came in the last months of her life after her youngest son, Gershom Whitfield, had been accepted for missionary service. But how could he leave his mother? He might never see her again. He would have delayed his departure, but his mother's words were a loving correction:

> My son, do you so little know your mother? Do you not realise that it is my ambition, my heart's desire, to see you all, every one of my children, serving the Lord where the need is greatest? I would not keep you back one hour.

Nor did she. Only a few months after Gershom had sailed for China, Fanny Guinness left behind her weakness and limitations for ever. On 3 November 1898 she was welcomed home at last to that city 'which has foundations, whose builder and maker is God'.

Notes

1. During its first thirty years Harley Institute had trained 887 men and 281 women, sending 215 missionaries to Africa, 182 to Asia, 172 to the Americas and others to some of the earth's remotest regions.
2. He would gain an honorary doctorate and Fellowship of the Royal Astronomical Society.
3. A premillennialist, Henry Guinness took a *continuous historicist* view of the book of Revelation, believing it was possible to match up various political events that had taken place with the prophecy that had foretold them. Based on the interaction between lunar and solar cycles, he did actually correctly predict both the creation of a national homeland for the Jews in 1917 (he himself died in 1910) and 1948 as a year of high significance for the Jewish people; in fact it was the year when the independent state of Israel was created.

Suggestions for further reading

John Foxe

But God, John Foxe and his Work, D. C. Relf, Gospel Magazine Trust, 2005. Introductory essays to copies of *Book of Martyrs*.

Paul Greenwood and Jonathan Maskew

Methodist Heroes in the Great Haworth Round, J. W. Laycock, Keighley, 1909; *Lives of Early Methodist Preachers,* Thomas Jackson, vol. 4, 1873; *William Grimshaw of Haworth,* Faith Cook, Banner of Truth Trust, 1997.

Susanna Harrison

Short introduction to *Songs in the Night,* 1823.

Gerhard Tersteegen

Recluse in Demand, Lillian Harvey; and *Sermons and Hymns,* Harvey and Tait, Stoke-on-Trent, UK.

Isabella Graham

The Power of Faith, Life and Writings of the late Mrs Isabella Graham, New York, 1816.

Hugh Bourne

Memoirs of the Life and Labours of Hugh Bourne, John Walford, Reprinted, Tentmakers Publications, 1999; *The Romance of Primitive Methodism,* Joseph Ritson, 1909.

John Gifford

John Bunyan, his Life, Times and Work, John Brown, 1885; *Fearless Pilgrim, the life and times of John Bunyan,* Faith Cook, EP, 2008.

Fanny Guinness

The Guinness Legend, Michele Guinness, Hodder & Stoughton, 1990; *Guinness of Honan,* Mrs Howard Taylor, CIM, 1930; *Lucy Guinness Kumm,* Henry Grattan Guinness, 1907.